FAT,
FAME
and LIFE
with FATHER

FAT,
FAME
and LIFE
with FATHER

Deirdre Barnard

DOUBLE
STOREY
a juta company

First published 2003 by Double Storey Books,
a division of Juta & Co. Ltd,
Mercury Crescent, Wetton, Cape Town

ISBN 1-919930-34-5

Thanks to David Kramer for permission
to quote from 'Skipskop'

Page design by Sarah-Anne Raynham
Page layout by Claudine Willatt-Bate
Cover design by Toby Newsome
Printing by Interpak, Pietermaritzburg

For my mother

Every family needs a solid foundation on which to build its hopes and dreams. And it needs a secure refuge when the inevitable buffeting of life puts these hopes and dreams in jeopardy.

Our family has had its fair share of turbulence, and through all the rough times my mother has been just such a rock. When things have been bad, even when she has been worst affected, she has made it her priority to be there for those closest to her: me, my brother and our respective families.

My mother is courageous and steadfast, and sometimes I think she doesn't know how much I admire those qualities in her. There are times, I'm sure, when I haven't been exactly the kind of daughter she might have expected, but she has always been exactly the mother I would have wanted. It could never have been any other way.

For all that she is, for giving me life, for celebrating my successes and for offering me – without question – a safe haven when things haven't gone well, I acknowledge and thank her. And at the end of it all there is only one thing to be said:

'Dankie, Mamma, vir alles. Ek is lief vir jou.'

CONTENTS

Foreword

Why did I enjoy reading this book so much?

Was it the pleasure of reliving experiences I had been privileged to participate in at the time, of reading afresh anecdotes that I had enjoyed before, or of discovering new ones? Or was it learning that Professor Barnard had obtained as much personal satisfaction from the projects completed through the Christiaan Barnard Foundation during his last years as I had?

I have known the Barnards for over fifteen years and can testify to the fact that Deirdre, like her father before her, is a natural storyteller. She has a flair for conveying the emotional truth of a situation, and her deep love of children – something she shared with her father – shines through this book.

Deirdre's journey has not always been easy. One can only admire the way in which she has turned difficult personal situations into stepping stones towards a greater insight into life. Maybe it is the delightful sense of humour that she brings to both the ups and the downs of existence that enables her to take the positive from every situation and leave the negative behind her.

Susan Vosloo
Cardio-Thoracic Surgeon, Christiaan Barnard Memorial Hospital

My life so far

1950 Born on 28 April
1951 My brother Andre born on 30 March
1961 Move to Zeekoevlei
      Enter my first international waterskiing competitions
      in France and Spain
1965 Ranked second in the world at championships in
      Australia
1967 My father performs the first heart transplant on
      3 December
      My last year of school
1969 My first year at the University of Stellenbosch
      My parents divorce
1970 My father marries Barbara
1971 My first cruise
1973 Become Mej. Viets
      Become a Hyde Park nanny
1975 Become a governess
      Begin teaching
1978 Marry Kobus Visser
1980 First child, Karen, born on 15 July
1982 Second child, Tiaan, born on 17 July
1983 Ninon boutique opens
      My father and Barbara divorce
1984 Andre dies
1988 My father marries Karin
1998 Barbara dies
1989 Purple rain in Greenmarket Square
1990 Release of Mandela
1994 First democratic elections – beginning of the 'New'
      South Africa
2000 My father and Karin divorce
2001 My father dies on 2 September

Introduction

Did you know that when Holden Caulfield starts relating *The Catcher in the Rye* he's actually writing everything down for a psychiatrist? I didn't know this until someone told me, but I do understand why he was doing it.

I am not against psychiatrists. I think that sometimes, given the things that happen to you, there's nothing like a brainwash to sort it all out. Analysis paralysis is what I don't like. By which I mean that psychiatrists are only people, after all. They do the best they can with the raw material they get given and after that it's up to you to get on with your life.

I don't know about Holden. I just hope things worked out all right for him in the end. But I think his psychiatrist had the right idea. Maybe he couldn't tell him where the ducks go in the winter, but sometimes it helps just to write things down and get them on paper all neat and tidy and accounted for, and then you can put them all behind you and move forwards.

I know, because I have learnt the value of writing things down.

I don't want to wait until I'm dead for someone to say things about me and then get the story all wrong. If this is what should happen to me, there is no guarantee that I wouldn't end up like poor Elvira in Noël Coward's *Present Laughter* and have to come back as a ghost and get in everyone's way and chip in, because I am a great chipper-in. So before that happens, I think it's better if I take the opportunity and just put down My Life So Far, which by and large has not been too bad.

I've had plenty of good times. I've learnt a few lessons. I'm old enough now to have a few ideas of my own about things and until very recently I thought I'd keep those to myself. Or maybe, I thought, when I was a very old lady and not just auditioning for the job as I sometimes feel I am now, I'd put it all down in one of those old school exercise books we had to go out and buy before first term at school.

In the end I decided to do it now. I sat down and began to write and now, whenever anyone comes to the house, I just push the exercise book out of the way or under a pile of magazines because what I don't want is for someone to say: 'Hey, Deirdre, what's that? What are you writing?'

You may be too polite to ask that kind of question, but all that means is that you're the exception. During the course of my life people, sometimes people I don't even know, have come up to me and asked me the kinds of questions you'd never even ask your best friend. So I have learnt to be careful. I keep the things I really think, to myself. Also, I feel a bit awkward. I am a bit Barnard-conscious. I know the kinds of things people say about the Barnards. '*Kry ons nooit ent met hierdie Barnards nie?* When are we going to see the end of these Barnards?' and 'What's her claim to fame after all? She was only Chris Barnard's daughter.'

In one way they're right. But it isn't the easiest thing in the world to have had a parent who's been on the cover of *Time*. And in another, far more important way, they're absolutely wrong. I've been many things in my life but only Chris Barnard's daughter was never one of them, and I think right here, before we go any further, there is something I ought to say about writing about your life.

My father wrote his book *One Life* with a writer called Curtis Bill Pepper: this was his side of the story. A lot of pressure was put on my mother to have her say, and in a book titled *Heartbreak* she did. I never read either of these books and I'll tell you why. I'm a remedial teacher. Children are my special field of interest and when a child comes to me 'new' from some other school, or for private remedial tuition, they always come with a 'history'. Usually it comes in a regulation beige file that is handed over to you along with the child. Children aren't stupid. They know it's their life that's in the file and you can see in their eyes what they think. They think you've already made up your mind about them, so what chance have they now to show that they're so much more than whatever other people have made of them?

I don't read those children's files. I like to form my own opinions and so far it has worked very well for me. In fact, it's worked wonders. This is why it's so nice sometimes to pass the time with complete strangers. They have no preconceptions about you. Fame and a public face may be addictive to some people: the truth is that anonymity also has its charms.

The story of a doctor achieving international success, of a betrayed and badly hurt wife and all that came after, even when told by two of the major actors, was of no real interest to me. It may seem a strange thing to say, but the various published versions of this story had very little to do with my life.

Real life dramas take place in real life, not in the pages of newspapers or books. The best you can expect from a re-telling is just another version of what happened. When it comes to my own life, I like to make up my own mind. I don't want to read someone else's account of it. Not my father's, not my mother's and certainly not anyone else's.

My story – which is rather too small to need a grand hook like 'autobiography' to hang itself from – is just another version of some lives already told. There will be some people in it you know and some whom you've probably never heard of before. I hope there may be some kind of 'wisdom' here too, just some stuff that got picked up along the way, which would go to show that at the end of all the good times and bad times there was something of value in all that had happened.

Anton Chekhov had what he called 'autobiographophobia'. To prove his point he once wrote a one-paragraph autobiography, which he thought more than sufficient. He also said he 'kept back from his stories the images and scenes dear to me … which I have treasured and kept carefully hidden'. I understand this. Everyone is entitled to some things that belong only to them, and if they're to stay precious then it has to be that way.

In writing your own story, it is so easy to present yourself in a favourable light. In the end it is a bit like eating Ferrero Rocher chocolates more than one at a time: there's something guiltily self-indulgent about it. But after a while I realised that it wasn't just myself I was writing about. I was writing about other people too, who had the same things happen to them as happened to me. And there was a lot of comfort in that. I didn't feel quite so peculiar any more. What I felt was liberated.

Looking back over what I have written in these pages, I could say that my story is about the girl I once was and the woman I became and the things that have happened. And while on the one hand some of it made me heartsore, on the other hand most of it has really been rather wonderful.

I wouldn't wish anyone the bumpy parts, although we all know that if there's one thing we can depend on it's that some time or other, they will surely come our way. I like to concentrate on how we cope, what we learn and how there's something wonderful in the overall balance, which always leaves us a bit richer and more well-rounded as a person than we were before.

So this book really isn't about me at all. Well, it is and it isn't. It's about how my life happened to be but it's also for anyone who has ever been fat, affected in one way or another by divorce, or dreamed about how it might be to wake up one morning and find they were Hollywood swimming star Esther Williams or Flipper the Dolphin.

It's about being a parent and being a child. It's about love, which is to say it's also about loss. It's about the myth that surrounds stepmothers and about the best way to lose weight really fast, which involves no food at all and lots of black coffee. It's about things that are really bad for you and some things that are really good. Like cruising, by which I mean on the P&O liner *Oriana*, and not working your way up and down Burg Street after midnight on Saturday.

It's about Andy Warhol and his fifteen minutes of fame. How much do we want it and, if it should come our way, what kind of price would we be willing to pay for it?

When I was at school struggling with compositions my father, who couldn't stand to see anyone suffer – never mind me in my school uniform with my pencil in my mouth, looking desperately for words – offered me some advice. He gave me a 'one size fits all' solution as far as any piece of writing is concerned, which worked very well for me. He could never see the point of people wasting time. He said if I just wrote down, 'The great grey clouds rolled over and the heavy drops of rain began to fall' and took it from there, I'd be fine.

It made sense to me. Everyone has to begin somewhere. So this is what I did, and it worked for topics as diverse as 'A Day at the Seaside', 'What I Hope to Be when I Grow Up' and even 'The Person in History I Most Admire'. So I think what I'll do is stick to the maybe useful stuff and just focus on that and so here – and not in any particular order, and any way you like it – we go.

'The great grey clouds rolled over and the heavy drops of rain began to fall …'

The fat thing

… or why has Oprah not yet
replied to my e-mail on the subject
and invited me to be on her show?

I decided I would start with the 'fat thing' because this is the thing that seems to worry so many people. I don't mind talking about it because it's something I know about. I've been fat and then thin and then fat again. I have photographs to prove it.

In March 1973 I was on the cover of the *Foto-Rapport* wearing a yellow bikini. In the photograph I am standing with one thigh squeezed against the other, trying to make both thighs look smaller. This is because I was 'Mej. Viets', which I see (because I have just looked it up in the *Tweetalige Skoolwoordeboek*, the bilingual school dictionary) means 'smart, spruce or dapper'.

I don't think I look 'smart, spruce or dapper'. I think I look like an overweight girl sucking in her stomach and trying to hide those unfortunate thighs.

How, you might ask, did I get to be Mej. Viets? The answer is that the newspaper *Rapport* was running a weight-loss competition. There were lots of wonderful prizes to be had. In fact, there were so many you might almost call it an embarrassment of riches, but there was only one I really wanted and that was the round-the-world trip on the *Oriana*.

If you entered you had to lose weight while using Annetjie Theron's product Wonderslim, and I did. I also forsook all my bad habits, or as many as I could. I bought myself a pink bicycle and cycled to university.

I wanted that trip really badly. In fact, I wanted it so badly I even had some base thoughts about it. While I was huffing and puffing, trying to burn up calories just as fast as I could on my pink bicycle, I wondered whether being Prof. Barnard's daughter might not be good for something after all. I don't know if it helped. Perhaps it did. In any case, I won, and if you look at some of the pictures from that time, some of the contestants who didn't quite make it aren't exactly looking at me with love in their eyes!

Nevertheless, I'd done all that was asked of me. I did take Annetjie Theron's Wonderslim, I stuck to the diet, I cycled my heart out and I won the trip I'd so badly wanted.

I also got to share the same edition of *Foto-Rapport* with a pin-up of a musician called Dimpel Pretorius, because in those days people like that really existed and found their way into the media (which only means, come to think of it, that the media hasn't changed all that much).

What was important is that we were going to New Zealand, Fiji, Honolulu, Hawaii, Vancouver and San Francisco, before ending up in New York with a screen test and the possibility of a brilliant career in the movies.

I had a 'princess' called Topsie Koekemoer, a housewife from Lichtenburg, who came second. I won a Chevrolet, Topsie and I each won a stove from CJ Fuchs and Topsie won an outfit worth R250,00. (I don't know what you could buy with that money back then, today I would have spent all mine on those Ferrero Rocher chocolates. You just have to remember this was a long time ago.)

There were seven of us altogether. One of the others was called

Queenie Roets. I suppose she got her stove along with the rest, but besides that all she got was R50,00 for an outfit. In the picture in the *Foto-Rapport* she looks very *dikbek* about it, very disgruntled, and I can't say I blame her. Whichever way you look at it, R50,00 doesn't take you very far, not even in those days, and losing weight isn't easy.

I don't want to list the names of the others. They are probably all glamorous grandmothers by now. They probably went on the Mayo Diet years ago and stuck with it. Or they've all read *Fit for Life* and are eating sensibly now and jumping up and down to the Jane Fonda workout tapes and they're all thin as rails and all their friends are green with envy and wonder how they do it. I am sure they have put those fat girl days far behind them forever, and I'm glad if they have.

As for me, being fat or thin isn't the big thing the people around me once made it out to be. I have discovered pants with elastic tops and learnt that the older you get, the more funny it seems that once upon a time it all seemed so important.

So, what was it with the weight? I told you that people ask me things, and over the years this is one of the things I've been asked the most. How does an athlete competing at international level the way I was suddenly balloon the way I did? The answer is that it's not easy.

In the first place it doesn't happen all that suddenly. First of all you go through the bit where your clothes, especially trousers, seem to shrink slightly every time they go in the wash. Then you get that feeling that there has to be kryptonite or something somewhere, or the Bermuda Triangle's closer than it seems to be in the atlas, because every time you jump on a scale it goes funny.

It feels as if you wake up one morning and you're fat. The truth is it takes a bit longer than that. It takes a lot more effort, but don't turn the page because the word 'effort' gives you the *skriks*; don't be alarmed. We're not talking the kind of effort that means you have to take out a membership at the nearest health and fitness centre. This is a different kind of effort altogether, and I'll tell you exactly what it is. To get fat you have to eat. Preferably you have to eat a very great deal and at least some of it should be made up of things you know perfectly well are going to push up the kilograms and aren't in the least good for you.

If you want to be healthy, look wonderful and radiate good health and happiness, this section of the book isn't for you. Instead you should be reading *Fifty Ways to a Healthy Heart*, written by a doctor of good reputation – it comes highly recommended. Or you could log onto www.askbarnard.com, which has nothing directly to do with me, although I don't mind giving advice if you ask me and if that's the way you choose to go it will cost you nothing at all, but I talk a lot so you have to have time. (In case you're wondering, yes, the book and the website were both my father's, and both are still available.)

You don't get fat eating lots of fruit, vegetables and fish, enjoying bouzouki music, throwing the odd plate around out of pure zest for life and generally living in the Cretan way, which is the way recommended in the book mentioned above.

I got fat because I ate too much. Everyone seems to have their own ideas about why this was and I suppose there's a little bit of truth and a little bit of speculation in just about all of them.

People comfort eat when they're miserable about something. I've done that. I understand it. There are plenty of places to go if eating away your sorrows is what you're into. Bacon sandwiches, *boerewors* rolls, a whole slab of 'glass-and-a-half' Dairy Milk chocolate – you name it. Life isn't all beer and skittles, and plenty of us go through phases like this. But if you're feeling down, forget about food if you can and take comfort from this instead. At the end of it all these things either pass or we learn to live with them, and when the time comes to reclaim and take control of our lives, we can take control of our eating patterns too.

In my own case, quite a few things hit me at once. I don't think coming off the really tough regimen that goes with being an international waterskier helps. Once you drop that kind of discipline and sample freedom for what feels like the first time in your life it can be a pretty intoxicating feeling, and I celebrated it by eating whatever I could lay my hands on.

'What about your parents' divorce?' people say. They always say this. To some people, emotional upheaval and the private matter of two people heading towards a divorce that got rather too much public attention are far more interesting than the fact that putting on weight can result from a Pick 'n Mix bowl of reasons.

It's true that my parents weren't going through the happiest days of their marriage at that time and yes, I wasn't exactly throwing cartwheels for joy in the street. I was sad in the way you're sad when something strikes at the very heart of your world. Yes, a nice chocolate pudding or a big slice of cake probably did help and that may have been part of the reason: it all added up to the same thing. But my parents, even with their relationship falling apart all around them, were still my parents, and they were both horrified by what was happening to me.

The more horrified they were, the more I ate. I know what you're going to say. You'll say, 'She was doing it to spite them, to get their attention,' 'The poor girl had an eating disorder and just won't admit it.' I've had problems with eating, that's true, but there's something else you should know about this poor girl. I have even bigger problems than eating my way out of the blues. I have a very big *hardegat* problem, which is what the more refined English call hardboiled, and that's a good enough translation for a book suitable for reading by the entire family. There's nothing that makes me more determined to do something than when someone says I ought not to be doing it.

My sporting achievements had demanded very high levels of

discipline. (Sport was also good for my self-esteem. It wasn't until many years later that I learnt that some boys actually kept photographs of me as pin-ups, which is very funny when you come to think of it.) Once the constraints of keeping in training to participate in sport at an international level were removed, a whole range of new possibilities opened to me. Not only did I not have to get up at the crack of dawn every morning to practise and not only did I now not have to practise every day of my life, but I could also stop watching my diet. I could eat what I liked.

My parents were not very keen on either self-indulgence (that's the Calvinist thing – see Chapter 15) or overweight (because they thought it unhealthy), and 'plump and jolly' somehow seemed to them the sign of a life spent having too much of a good time. Needless to say, the more it upset them, the more determined I was to continue munching my way happily along the plump and jolly road.

Anyone who has ever had to deal with a teenager who has a mind of her own and her heels well and truly dug in will know exactly what I mean. Ask me, I have a daughter and so I know, and I can tell you first-hand now what I couldn't possibly have told you then.

My poor, long-suffering mother tried to run a household devoid of the kinds of food that should come with a Serious Temptation warning right next to the sell-by date. She managed to turn the house into a minefield for me by carefully secreting away things meant for guest consumption only, for which read sweets, biscuits and other forbidden foods. All *that* did was help me develop the ability to find what was forbidden with the kind of homing instinct a French truffle pig might have envied.

This is nothing new. It's the story of anyone who's ever wrestled with a weight problem and all of you out there who know about it know about it, and you don't need me to tell you, but there are some other things too.

People with yo-yo weight tend to have problems that go back a long way and no, I'm not going to get Jungian on you. Our family has been amateur-analysed so many times and so many people have come up with their own diagnoses that it's really not worth going back there. Anyway, it's history I want to tell you about, not psychology. I'd like to share another piece of Barnard business that as far as I know has never appeared in a newspaper or been disclosed in an interview.

You see, I do listen to people who say: 'For goodness sake, Deirdre, what can you possibly have to say that anyone hasn't heard at least a dozen times before?'

The story is this.

When I was small my mother, my brother and I were the camp followers. My father was the important one. Wherever he went for his work, we went along like a little gypsy troupe tagging behind.

This is just one of those many other things I now realise I wasn't alone in.

Any children out there with an ambitious, upwardly mobile father? You have to go where Dad's job takes you? Dad

(a) works long hours?
(b) is away on business trips such a lot that the dog no longer recognises him?
(c) is preoccupied with some world-shaking problem he just thinks he might have the solution to?

I can tell you all about this and so could my parents, and if you are one of these children your parents probably could too, although I think you'll hear two very different kinds of stories, the Dad one and the Mum one. You may just as well listen to both of them so that as you grow up, you learn to keep an open mind when you think back and remember how it was then. They're the kind of story that make my Camel-smoking, free-spirited daughter raise her eyebrows right up to the ceiling and wonder what it was all of us women were thinking back then.

Still, that's the way it was. Women went wherever their husbands went for their work and one of the places we went was into the doctors' residence at the old City Hospital in Cape Town. City Hospital was the city's infectious diseases hospital. It's a medical museum today, situated not far from the famous V&A Waterfront. There's a sign, but you probably drive right past it whenever you go in that direction and wouldn't even know it was there.

My father was making a study of tuberculous meningitis and was somewhere around the bottom rung of the ladder that would make him famous one day, but of course none of us could have known that then.

With my mother at the helm, my brother and I were getting along with the serious business of growing up to be Barnards and we were going to be good at it. My mother had decided that, probably at the moment of conception. My mother is a family maker and when she sets out to do something she gives it one hundred per cent commitment. When she does a thing, she does it well.

I bloomed like a cherub and unless you happen to be someone who's ever 'done' the churches and cathedrals of Europe and managed to find a cherub who could be classed as fashionably slender, you will know what I mean. I think now that perhaps this was the start of my problem.

In those early days at City Hospital, I was plump and jolly and self-satisfied too. My brother Andre, eleven months my junior (so you can see that my hard-working mother had her hands pretty full), wasn't as happy as I was. He wasn't as chubby either. My brother was a very small baby still keen on his bottles. He was certainly not old enough yet to be able to articulate his woes with anything but an outraged howl. In any event, he was – conveniently for me – still at that stage before he could verbalise. Even so, it all came out later. I regularly stole his bottle and drank his milk.

I don't know what this tells you about me and my later history of weight gain, but I set it down here in my own words so there's no possibility later of my saying: 'Excuse me, but I never said that.' You must make what you like of it.

In later years my father remembered those bottles, although not quite in the way we expected him to. When he married Barbara, after Frederick was born, he liked to tell people how Barbara fed the baby using brown, flat-sided medicine bottles instead of the more conventional kind.

It was a sensible thing to do. The baby lies down for his dinner and the bottle lies down flat next to him, except it wasn't Barbara who did this, it was my mother. That's what you get when you go right across the generation gap in search of a bride. By the time Barbara had her first child those flat-sided medicine bottles were history. The only place you'd find them now is probably in a museum rather like the one that stands on the site of the old City Hospital, in one of those exhibits where they recreate turn-of-the-century pharmacies.

People get things muddled sometimes and that's all right. There were occasions when he got the two later wives mixed up as well. Once in Greece when he was married to Karin, in a speech to an entire village, he thanked his wife 'Barbara' for her love and support. I suppose that's understandable too. Freudian slips happen. They happen to all of us. We all know they do but as far as I know, no matter how many other things he had on his mind, at no time in his life did he ever get my mother confused with anyone else. If you knew my mother, you'd understand why.

There's something else too, and while I'm getting things off my chest this might just as well come out. I have to say something about my mother's family. (I'm sorry Mamma / *Jammer, Ma.*) My mother comes from South-West African/Namibian farming stock.

Those kinds of people who work hard, sit out the droughts without complaint because they know it's God's will, and are the backbone of any country.

My Louw side, my mother's side, is like this, and in between doing all of these things, they enjoy their food. My father's family were poor people. They were grateful to have food on the table at all and hardly ever ate meat. His father was thin and so was his mother. When he said that at least in one way he was privileged in his childhood – in the sense that no one in his family had problems with weight, he never needed to go on a diet and that this very probably had something to do with his genes – this was true and he was lucky.

My mother comes from a good old-fashioned farming family. My father would never have put any of his patients on the kind of food my mother's family decked out their table with but I can tell you that that food really is wonderful. My mother can still make the best *vetkoek* with Lyle's golden syrup you've ever tasted in your life, and don't tell me how many smart restaurants you've been into, it makes no difference at all – believe me, you've never tasted anything like it. Unless you know my mother and she's ever made some for you, you'll just have to trust me on this.

I don't know. Perhaps it's something in the genes, but there are some very *fris*, that is, powerfully built, aunties on my mother's side. I was going to say that in English this means 'buxom', but I see that the *Tweetalige Skoolwoordeboek* says what it really means is 'hale and hearty', and so that is what those foremothers on my mother's side were like. Which, when you come to think about it, should hardly come as any great surprise. You can't tame a wild land like Namibia, which you could drop England into and not easily find again in a week, if you look like Kate Moss.

I don't know, but I don't think anyone ever said any of these women had an eating disorder, and my mother has the most beautiful figure. In those days, when my father first knew her and they fell in love, she was known to have 'the most beautiful eyes of any theatre sister in Groote Schuur Hospital, and the rest of her wasn't too bad either'. All the men could see of the theatre sisters was their eyes looking out over the masks and their ankles sticking out under the surgical gowns and Groote Schuur is a big hospital, so it's a big compliment and my mother deserves it.

My mother tackled my fat problem her way and my father, who also didn't think my piling on the kilos was such a great idea, did it in his. Because he had a scientific turn of mind, he thought a 'monitored eating programme' was what I needed to put things right and arranged for me to be admitted to Groote Schuur Hospital and put on one.

'You're going,' he said. 'No arguments.'

'Fine,' I said. 'I'll go.'

You know how it is when you say one thing and are thinking something else altogether? That's how I said it, but I went, and when I checked in I took my 'attitude' with me. The truth is that I will go anywhere. I have an adventurous spirit and wherever I go I take my 'attitude' with me and my 'attitude' then was a lot less tame than it is now.

I'd like to just say something about attitude, and it's this. Attitude can work for you or against you. Which way it goes is up to you. As far as weight loss or gain is concerned, ultimately you call the shots and here's some advice and it comes free of charge. Being your own worst enemy is not such a great idea. It tends to be rather a turn-off. People are almost certain not to feel one bit sorry for you, so you end up feeling sorry for yourself. Which is just about the silliest, loneliest 'nowhere' place in the world to be, and you do not have to go there.

My father worked at Groote Schuur Hospital. It was like my second home and I had a wonderful stay there. I am grateful to my father for setting it all up for me but not even he, with all his degrees, awards and honours, had made proper allowance for a chocolate dispensing machine in the foyer. Besides which, I am the kind of person who can set up camp just about wherever I happen to find myself. I make friends easily and a hospital is a wonderful place to meet new people and hear new stories. Why else do you think *E R* and *St Elsewhere* are so popular? And we won't even talk about *Scrubs*.

There were plenty of people sorry for the daughter of the hard-hearted doctor who acted so determined to get his daughter slimmed down. The staff were very nice and so were the other patients and they kept passing on to me all that stuff their visitors kept bringing them to eat, because everyone knows how terrible hospital food is. I don't think I'd ever had it so good. Certainly not at home, where my mother saw everything and didn't miss a trick.

I just kept eating away, and in a way it made me feel good. When you're young you take a perverse delight in beating the system. (See 'your own worst enemy' above.) It's a bit self-defeating, I know, but you only find that out when you get older. Of course the treatment didn't work and my mother kept trying to do things her way and my father tried again too.

He sent me to Forest Mere in Sussex, England – a very smart place that was certainly one jump ahead of the old chocolate machine trick. It was an expensive treat. Now I know that 'treat' might not be how everyone sees this. I have told you that people ask me things they'd never in a hundred years ask anyone else, and questions about being sent to Groote Schuur to lose weight and even being 'exported' to Forest Mere are among them. More pressure from the parents is what they seem to think was happening here, and didn't I mind? Wasn't I devastated? Did I feel they wanted this new, fat, unacceptable daughter simply to vanish and be replaced by the skinny little girl I'd once been? The truth is that it wasn't like that.

Children have 'phases'. I was having one, defiantly and happily eating everything I hadn't had time to eat before in those not-so-long-ago yesterdays when food was really only important as fuel to keep my body at the level of fitness it had to be. Now I was free to have a good time and pig out, if you like to put it that way, and my parents weren't punishing me, they were trying to help.

I knew that and was appreciative of it. My father wanted me to be thinner for my own sake. He wanted me to be able to fit into nice clothes again and feel good in them, and trust me on this, Forest Mere is not what anyone could possibly call a penitentiary. It's a wonderful place and although it wasn't the home from home that Groote Schuur hospital had been, I made friends there too. I met some very nice young men from Saudi Arabia and they had a car and we weren't all that far from a very nice town, and it's not so hard to guess what happened next. The end result was that the scale stayed exactly where it always stayed. The only way you could have made it move was to hit it hard with a crowbar.

My visit to Forest Mere was not the conspicuous success my parents hoped it would be, but it didn't stop them trying. In those days 'Jack Flax' injections were supposed to be exactly the thing to do the trick. You had to fly to Johannesburg to get them and my father arranged for me to do this.

I think now that the injections were probably water but there was a special diet you had to stick to that went along with them. I stuck to the diet and I lost weight. This was in the days just before I started university, and thanks to Jack Flax and because for a change I listened to someone else, when I registered as a first-year student I didn't stick out because of my weight. I could blend in, and I needed that then.

I've always liked anonymity. I like places that give me the freedom to be myself and say what I like and not feel guilty when the things that jump out of my mouth before I can stop them are hanging around out there in the open.

I suppose you could say that Stellenbosch was a good place to be at that time of my life. University is a great leveller of people. Everyone's the same there. No one is really interested in what's going on with your father or whether or not your parents are divorcing. Young people are selfish that way. Someone else's business is never quite as interesting as their own and because I'd been having a bit of a bumpy ride round about then, for me that was quite a relief. My only wish was that it could have been like that everywhere and stayed like that forever.

I will say more about myself as a Fat Lady later in the book and how I managed to 'cure' it, for a little while anyway, by cruising; and also how it came back and was all that stood between me and a promising career in films.

I also have some useful tips for instant weight loss that might catapult you into international travel and adventure like they did me. Unfortunately they involve diuretics ('water loss' medication) and laxatives (not for nothing am I a doctor's daughter), but you will not be able to take advantage of them without first consulting your doctor and I can tell you right now what they'll say. They'll say it's just about the worst idea they've ever heard in their life and whoever put such a thought into your head should try being less irresponsible.

What I would say to anyone who's been where I have with the weight thing is not to focus too much on food. It's easy for thin people to say: 'Oh, if only they'd just eat properly.' I have great sympathy for and empathy with people who are fat, because no one knows better than I do that you have to get your mind right before you can lose weight.

At this stage of our lives we all know what to eat to get thin. Food is a part of life. It's there to be enjoyed. The trick is to eat small quantities. Dress them up to the nines with sprigs of anything you can lay your hands on so they look as if they come straight from Lutèce in New York, because this will make them look more generous, but just keep them small.

One final thing I can also tell you (and I will, except later, not now) is how to get the optimum reading out of any scale ever invented with the minimum inconvenience to yourself, although this involves a massive cruise liner and a heavy mid-Atlantic swell.

Which means that perhaps we should go from here to that part of my life during which I fell deeply in love with cruising, cruise ships and all that goes with them.

2

Cruising

*Not the kind that happens at Angels
or at the Bronx or on Saturday
nights in Burg Street*

I like cruising. If I have a choice I like cruising on a P&O liner, because who is there with a soul so dead that they can resist the notion of going cruising with a company that started its life as the Peninsular and Oriental Steam Navigation Company? I don't care how much you know of the world or of travel. That is glamour and real glamour is not a thing you get cut-price off the shelves in the Wal-Mart store.

I want you to know, by the way, that P&O pay me nothing to make such a fuss about how wonderful they are. I have sampled the goods and that's my own private opinion, given free and unsolicited.

For me cruising is the cure for all ills. I know it's an escape from reality, but at the time in my life when I was so mad about it, I did not know where my niche in life lay, as is often the case with young people. Escaping reality for a while suited me just fine.

Yachts are always called the toys of the rich, but at the end of it all I suppose being rich is like being thin. It's very nice but it isn't the answer to everything (which doesn't mean you should give up and stop trying). Wallis Simpson, the Duchess of Windsor, said you could never be too rich or too thin. She was both and even so it never got her what she really wanted, although I suppose you have to take into account that what she wanted was to be Queen of England, and that's really a very great deal to ask: it doesn't matter how thin you may be.

Aristotle Onassis was as rich as can be but his life wasn't a bed of roses even though he had the *Christina* to sail his troubles away in. Goodness knows it didn't do much for his daughter. Even though she had a boat with her name on it, it didn't help much, not in the weight department or any other department either.

It's nice to think that jumping on a cruise liner can be the cure for all ills. I still propagate that idea, although I know better, but even if it isn't a cure it's still a wonderful way to spend time. I have to admit that, whichever way you look at it, ships are seductive to me.

When my father was feeling so low when the divorce from his last wife, Karin, was happening, I told him I had the answer for him. What he ought to do is just make up his mind, go out and buy a couple of tickets, take Maureen Brink – his good friend of the old days – with him, get on the *QE2* and go right round the world.

I don't suppose I helped matters by telling everyone that I'd decided that Maureen was going to be his fourth wife. I don't think he was in the mood for any more wives at that stage, but of course that didn't keep me quiet.

'You should think about it,' I said, only half-joking. 'You've known her forever, she's wonderfully good looking, she'll take care of you and if you want to gallivant with the young girls I'm sure she won't mind.'

It didn't go down very well, but no one can say I didn't try. If you said to me now, 'Come on, Deirdre. Let's jump on a boat and go on a nice cruise somewhere,' I would be packing my suitcase before you even finished the sentence, but when I put this suggestion to my father he wasn't in the frame of mind to pay it much attention. He knew that something as simple as booking himself on a cruise was not the answer for him. I wish for his sake it had been that easy, but the truth is that he was a very sad man. He grieved for the loss of his young family and I knew, because life had taught me by now, that there is, in this world, no quick fix for the way he was feeling.

In fact, it was my father who introduced me to cruising. He invited me to go along with him and his second wife, Barbara, on the *Chusan* on a trip to South America. It was a huge excitement for me.

On that first *Chusan* cruise I was still in my fat phase, but when I look back now at photographs of that time, I don't know what I was so self-conscious about. I wasn't a string bean but *ek het darem nie te bad gelyk nie* – I didn't look too bad. And anyway, someone once said it isn't just the looks or the kilograms, it's the personality that counts. Personality was a very big thing in those days. There was a song about it and even a magazine named after it, and I think it's true: a pleasant personality can take you a very long way.

In those bad last days of my Dad – when, before I could bite off my tongue and stop the words jumping out, I said he looked like the Elephant Man – he still had personality. People would stop him on the street to talk to him – they always did that – and even when he looked his worst he was always willing to stop and chat, and he wasn't a fool. He could see that people took notice of what he looked like and were probably thinking: '*Haai*, shame, and he was such a nice looking man in his day.'

He talked his way through it. If you were with him you could actually see him doing it and he was able to do that, just as he always had been, because no matter how he looked, he was still himself. Only the outside had changed and it was the inside people responded to. I suppose in a way some of them might have missed that old glamorous package, but no one ever went away after speaking to him feeling unsatisfied or let down.

I knew why it was like this. I like people too and get along well with them. The good, the bad and the ugly, it's all the same to me. I've never met a person yet who hasn't got some fabulous gift to bring to the party of life, if you're only willing to take a bit of time to listen.

This was the approach to life that I took along cruising with me and I became convinced of something else, which is this. For very little input on my side, really just by being there and being myself and not bothering to try to be all those many things I'm not, life could take me a very long way. I knew this before I ever went on that first cruise, but it was while I was on the *Chusan* that I had time to practise, if that's what you like to call it. Suddenly I was in a place full of interesting people, none of them sopping wet with skis on their feet, who didn't expect anything from me other than that I should be myself and join in the fun.

I suppose you could say that I was between lives at that time. My waterskiing days were behind me and university was on hold. I suppose these days I would have had a gap year in which to sta-bilise, find my bearings and seek out some sensible sort of direc-tion – although I might just have spent it having a very good time. Instead I went cruising and it seemed to me as if a whole new world was opening up.

So there I was on the *Chusan* with Barbara and my father, with my new 'cruise wear' in my suitcase, because I at least wanted to have the proper clothes so that I would look like something and not let the side down; and I was ready to go.

I didn't mind at all being the third spoke on the wheel. I was there, that's what counted. There are some things in life it's just as well to come to terms with. Up to a point and in a very small way I'd been the star in my own little show. My parents loved me. I'd had my name in the papers and some attention as a skier and it felt very good, but nothing lasts forever. You grow up, you move away, you move on. In a different way that was true for my father, but as it happened it was true for me too. Sometimes change hurts, but as there's not very much you can do about it, the best thing to do is accept it, learn to live with it and strike out as hard as you can in your own direction. Easy? Not always. Inescapable? Certainly.

As far as my father and Barbara and that voyage on the *Chusan* are concerned you don't have to be a genius to work out that there's only room for so many stars in a show and that in this particular show I wasn't going to be one of them. Which was something I could live with. I'd had my days in my rather damp spotlight when I was waterskiing and I was quite happy with that.

There was something else too. There comes a time in a girl's life when she discovers there are plenty of interesting men in the world and wonders why it is that her father, who she's known all her life, is suddenly being made such a big fuss of.

I mean, your father is your father is your father. In that way I'm not any different. I happened to be on the *Chusan*. All girls are in the same metaphorical boat. It doesn't matter if your father is a plumber or a road worker or a rocket scientist – unless something goes very badly wrong, for a long time he's the man at the centre of your world. It's his job. That's the way it works. Jung said so and if you don't believe Jung I suppose you can always log on to Oprah and ask Dr Phil. If you don't mind queuing up behind half of the rest of the world, that is.

Then things change and you have to let go. One minute you're a child and the next minute you aren't. I don't know how other young women feel about it but for me, with the skiing, the transplant and the change in our domestic life, which affected us all, it was a bit like bursting through the sound barrier. It was so quick, in the way that it always is when a life is turned upside down. It wasn't a bed of roses, but then change never is. I'm not going to make jokes about it because in this process of change, inevitably, there were people I loved who were hurt. They were what the Americans call collateral damage, and that may be all very well when you're sitting in the Pentagon Press Office cooking up phrases, but it's not very nice when you're down on the ground living them out. You do live it out, though. You go in one end, you come out the other and the you that comes out is probably a little bit different from the you that went in. I suppose I felt a great many things while I was taking that bit of a buffeting, but by the time I came out of it, stood myself up, dusted myself off and thought about it, the overwhelming thing that I felt was relief. In a funny kind of way I was free. I could go back to a far more real world than the one I'd just come from. I could be just like other young women. I could be 'normal'.

I knew it would come, all the dating business and meeting nice men and having them make a fuss of you and wanting to take you out and so on. What I didn't know is how nice it would be. To which I suppose you will say: 'Hello, and where exactly had she been until then?'

The truth is I'd been skiing. I'd been doing 'things in a crowd'. I was in a single-sex residence at the University of Stellenbosch, where you had a curfew time if you went out at night and there was a House Mother in charge who kept an eye on you the same way your own mother would, except worse.

I hadn't been on a cruise liner with the sun in the morning and the stars in the evening and the moon at night. I hadn't been on a boat full of people with their hearts set on nothing but having a good time.

On that first cruise, my dad and Barbara and I were invited to sit at the Captain's table. We were asked if we'd like to go up onto the bridge, and it was wonderful to me.

If you've spent most of your life on skis being dragged behind a small boat through freezing cold water, being on a big boat makes a massive and not at all unpleasant change. Instead of standing around with your teeth chattering trying to warm up on too-hot coffee, there always seems to be a waiter standing by right next to you, offering something nice to drink with a straw and a bit of fruit in it. You can lie in a deck chair while you enjoy it. The man steering the boat isn't yelling back at you telling you what you're doing wrong, and the last thing in the world you're worried about are the water conditions.

This is also the cruise on which I acquired my fascination with life below decks. I made some good friends among the passengers, people I keep in contact with to this day, although that cruise was a very long time ago. There were lots of lovely people – any number to choose from – but I liked the crew better. I don't know why. I don't think it really matters why. I just did. They used to have wonderful shows of their own put on by the gay crew members and everyone was roped in and those shows were as good as and probably sometimes even better than anything you would find in first class.

I think I'm a coalface person. The drinks at the Captain's table were wonderful but you can have enough of that too, if you know what I mean, and anyway, I always like to talk to everyone. I like to ask people their business – I am like that – and on a ship that means the cabin stewards and the ship's officers and the ship's entertainers, who are a bit like a travelling circus.

After all, if you count Water Year and skiing practically every dam in South Africa (which is not a country short on dams) I am an entertainer myself, so I felt at home. For those too young to remember, Water Year was declared some time in the early 1970s to make South Africans more aware of the importance of this scarce resource. As waterskiers – we were known as Aqua Stars – we were called upon to help promote water awareness.

Perhaps you could say that on board ship I found a place where I was really happy and I had the best time anyone could ask for.

If that ship turned into the *Marie Celeste*, destined to sail the oceans of the world forever and never reach port, that would have suited me just fine too, except of course it didn't happen like that. Eventually the cruise came to an end, as cruises must. Everyone was a bit sad, as people tend to be, but I was truly devastated.

I didn't even like the feel of my own hometown ground under my feet. Forget pancakes, I felt about as flat as a slice of matzos, and you can't get much flatter than that. I couldn't wait to go cruising again, but as I was very much a child of the water by this time and had been an Aqua Star in my day, I suppose this is hardly surprising.

My life as an Aqua Star

'Look, everyone, I can do this.'
The things a child will do to draw
attention to itself, and where they
might land up as a result

When I was a child we had the best family holidays anyone could possibly wish for – at least, that's how I remember it now. One of the places we went to was Hentie's Botel at Knysna.

Knysna, as you probably know, is a small town in South Africa's own Lake District. If you are driving to Knysna from Cape Town you pass the holiday village of Sedgefield, where later in my life my father and Barbara had a small farm. After Sedgefield the road runs along the crest of a line of low coastal hills, with the Indian Ocean on your right and a string of lakes on your left – jewel lakes that shine in the sun like a necklace, with rickety jetties that jut out over the water and small boats moored at the sides and hunched-over fishermen sitting all by themselves who never seem to catch anything. There are green hills on either side and beyond them, although you can't see it, is the sea.

Then there's the smell. This place has a wild smell all its own. People say it's the renosterbos and that may be so, but for me it doesn't really need any name. It carries in its heart the smell of my childhood, of holidays and of what it is to be carefree.

Off on these holidays we went, 'Mamma and Pappa and Boetie and me', all loaded up in the family car.

When you are a child you think that this wonderful time will last forever, that nothing will ever change. Your mother will have all her family together without all the demands of your father's hospital job. You will have your father's full attention. There will always be your brother sitting beside you in the back seat, close enough for a good squabble whenever you feel like it. There will be enough silly jokes and I Spy games and sing-songs to last all of your lifetime.

Is a memory something we've kept or something we've lost? I don't know the answer. All I know is that if I had known then what I know now, I would have tried with all my heart to remember those good times so that I could keep them quite perfect and hold onto them forever.

I must say one thing about my parents. During their time together they didn't have much money but even so, they managed to give us some wonderful holidays.

It was simple stuff but it was the most amazing fun. We stayed at Hentie's Botel. It was a very 'family' kind of place with family entertainment in the evening, and part of the entertainment was to put on a concert.

My father liked to play the role of a doctor with a patient all covered up. He did it in silhouette. He stood behind a white sheet with a light shining down on him, so all the audience could see was the shadow play.

He would ask for his 'instruments' and an assistant would pass him a huge spanner or a hammer, the most enormous tools, and all the while a narrator would be doing a funny voice-over.

I suppose it was, in its way, grotesque – a parody of all that was to come – but I sat there, a small barefoot girl, clapping and laughing along with the rest while the enormous silhouette wielded his huge, unsuitable tools over his invisible patient. Grand Guignol, I suppose it was, the kind of theatre that makes you laugh even as it makes you the slightest bit scared.

It all sounds very silly and small town now, but then we loved it and everyone roared with laughter.

Before Hentie's and holidays there was Christmas, so all through my childhood I had the feeling that all the good things came at once, packed together right next to each other at the end of the year.

Christmas but more especially Christmas Eve has always been a big thing in our family. My mother, who grew up in what was then German South-West Africa, followed the Christmas tradition of having the major Christmas celebration on Christmas Eve rather than on the day itself. There was always Father Christmas and he would miraculously find us wherever we happened to be. He might come on foot, by tractor or by speedboat, and he carried with him a little silver bell. Usually the bell stood in my mother's dining room, although ours wasn't exactly a house where you needed to ring for the next course, and no one questioned Father Christmas's right to appropriate it when he needed it!

Of course there were presents. Father Christmas carried a not unfamiliar pillow-case with him and after we'd sung Christmas carols together, the presents would be dished out from it.

All the men in our family had a turn to be Father Christmas and dress up in an old red gown with a cottonwool beard – my father, my brother, my brother's son Adam, my own son Tiaan and my husband Kobus too. In later years my sister-in-law Gail, who like my mother is a good seamstress, upgraded the outfit a bit.

My father loved being Father Christmas. One Christmas when I was a child and we were down at Buffels Bay for the holidays, we decided to extend our wonderful Christmas to others. That year my father had been given a gift of a huge quantity of sweets from a grateful patient who must have owned a sweet factory some-where. We decided we'd take the sweets, drive into the surround-ing area where there are some very poor people staying in the bush, and give our sweets to their children so they could have something special for Christmas as well.

Later Barbara introduced the German Christmas tradition to the family and sometimes it took quite delicate egg-dancing to keep everyone happy, but somehow we managed it.

These Christmases must have made a big impact on my father because when his third family came apart it was something he missed very much. His biggest wish was to go to their house and be Father Christmas again.

We were all going to Gail's house that last Christmas together and we decided that Kobus, who also had it in him to make magic for us, should do a reprise of his famous Father Christmas.

We hired a smart Father Christmas costume for him, with proper boots and a beard and a face mask and Kobus went off to make *the* visit to Armin and Lara. It was a big hit. My father was so happy and pleased at the way it went off: he couldn't stop talk-ing about the look of wonder and surprise on the children's faces. While he was expressing his delight in their pleasure I was looking at him. Our Christmases with him, my brother's and mine, when he had been a younger man, had been different. He had been vital then, at the very centre of things, but time had moved on. I could see it in his face and the way he moved his body and I felt a great tenderness towards him for all those things he must have known his other younger children would never know about him.

That Christmas meant a great deal to him – in fact, at that time, it meant just about everything. He came back positively beaming and talked about it for a long time afterwards.

It was at Hentie's that I discovered waterskiing, or perhaps you might say it discovered me. People came to Hentie's to ski the lake and of course it was inevitable that eventually someone should ask me if I'd like to try.

I did try and in that way kids have, I liked it, and then it got better than that. Some of the people who were out there watching the skiers said I had a talent for it. I thought that was marvellous. It's nice to have a talent for something and I think my parents were quite pleased too. It's reassuring for a parent when complete strangers come over and say: 'Is that your daughter out there on the water? It looks as if she can actually ski.' It makes you feel very pleased with yourself. It makes you want to get even better.

Then one summer the Cape Aquatic Club came to Hentie's. They were going to give a show there. They saw me ski and thought I had talent, and because if anyone should have known what they were talking about the Aquatic Club members should have, my parents began to sit up and take it more seriously.

This is where looking for attention and basking in praise leads you. This is how my life as an Aqua Star began, although if I had known then what I know now, I would probably have realised what was good for me and stayed on dry land, but I didn't do that.

My life was very ordinary then. We had lived all over the place, mainly to accommodate my father, his studies and his comings and goings when he was working and researching abroad.

After the skiing, things changed. Now we lived by the lake to accommodate me. My brother and I had to take the bus and then the train to get to school. I waterskied. My father worked at the hospital. My mother, who'd done lots of different jobs just to keep us all going while my father did all the preparatory work that would make him so famous one day, kept the whole thing together and we had what we wanted, which was an ordinary life.

Despite my success at waterskiing, that didn't change until my father 'went public'. He said himself that 'On Sunday I was a surgeon in South Africa, very little known. On Monday I was world-renowned.'

After that, we were never again going to be allowed what we in our family and what anyone in any normal, ordinary family would call a private life. Even my waterskiing was put under scrutiny.

To all those 'ordinary families' I would like to say one thing. Tolstoy was right when he opened *Anna Karenina* with one of the most famous first lines in the history of literature: 'All happy families are alike; each unhappy family is unhappy in its own way.' He knew what he was talking about. Value your 'alikeness', accept 'ordinariness' for the precious thing it is, because like so many things in life, you won't truly know what you have until one day you don't have it any more.

Once my father became 'the prominent cardiac surgeon' and 'the world's most respected doctor' and there were adjectives like 'world renowned' in front of his name, we lost our 'ordinariness'. Of course we were proud of him, but things changed for us and 'us' included me too and I hadn't expected that.

At that time my father and I were close. All of our family knew long before the big life change that he worked very long hours and that he worked hard. Our time together as a family was always hard-won. My time, by which I mean having my father to myself, was precious. It was wonderful we'd found something we could share. My achievements in waterskiing were what he called 'major highlights in my [i.e. his] life'. I liked them too. What I liked more is that they were something I could share with my dad.

He said I was too 'nice' to be a world champion. I was too good a loser. Do you think that's something I should mind very much? I don't mind being called 'nice'. It wasn't me who got a book review that said: 'For those interested in the story of a man with a long-lasting hunger to get to the top and whose appetite was satisfied, this book can be recommended.' That was my father, it wasn't me. If I ever wanted to be valued for anything at all it was for having done my best and having a good time while I was doing it, and I certainly had done so.

I think I should have stopped competitive waterskiing before I did. Perhaps I should have retired after the Australian trip, when I was second in the world, because that's when I peaked – but I didn't, and there's something else too. My father and I were a team. Everyone said we were a good combination. Once his life changed that particular partnership broke up. There were other people who could do the things that he'd done for me, but it could never have been the same. If I can make a comparison, it's like two dancers, say Fonteyn and Nureyev or Fred and Ginger. They could have danced and did dance with others, but without each other the magic was never really there.

That's how it was. At least, that's how it was for me. It's a funny thing. You never know when the last time will be. I can't remember now the last time I went out on the water with my father at the wheel of the boat. I suppose that when it's your life and happening to you and you're happy, you think it'll never end. You never think of the 'last time'. Yet, there always is 'a last time' – there has to be – and in my own case, I'm glad I don't remember the where and the when of it. Now, if I wish to, somewhere inside myself, I can always go back to those two people who don't exist any more. The small-town doctor at the wheel of the boat and the little waterskier, skimming over the water on a day that never changes somewhere in timelessness where conditions are just right and the moment is perfect.

But it ended. Of course it did. My waterskiing time had come to an end anyway. Competitive sport at this level is not something you do for too long out of your teens and my father's waterskiing coaching time had ended too. So in our different ways it was time for us to stop, it was right that we should have done so, and that's what happened.

~

For a year I skied professionally and got a chance to see a bit of the world. I got to see South Africa too. During the extravaganzas of Water Year I went out on the dams of South Africa with the rest of the team, raising 'water awareness' and wearing specially designed costumes Esther Williams would have killed for.

In terms of my everyday life, my father was 'out'. There were demands on him now that there had not been before and he lived a life separate and very different from our own. My mother, who in a sense took up where he left off, was very much 'in' and coming into her own in my waterskiing life. An Army Dakota flew the team all round the country for our aqua displays and my mother flew along with us, drinking whisky, playing cards (my mother is a ferociously competitive and really good card player) and generally being very popular with the grown-ups in the back of the plane.

My mother likes to gamble a little bit. She and our friends Father Tom and Dene Friedmann, who come into this story in more detail later on, used to go to the horse races together. She plays poker, one armed bandit and roulette.

My father said that a good poker player needs nerve and a straight face, much the same skills employed by any competent surgeon in an operating theatre. I suppose he should know, but if those are the criteria then I think that despite all the jobs my mother did to keep us all going – theatre sister, industrial nurse, secretary – perhaps she was still in the wrong job. If that really were what it took, she'd have been a wonderful surgeon.

If I have any regrets about my life at this time there can be only one really worth recording and that is that I was not allowed to be part of the water ballet. In the water ballet part of the pageant you were allowed to come out dressed like a ballerina in a tutu and it was decided by common consensus this could not be for me. I could be in the pyramid as long as I stayed at the end of the bottom line to provide a good strong shoulder to stand on and strong legs that would hold up. That was because I had begun to gain weight. First a little bit and then a little bit more and people had begun to notice.

All the same, thinking back now, I know I was fat but I don't think I looked too bad. There were lots of young boys around. In those days there were plenty of young men in the army doing their national service and most of them were in army camps in the back of beyond, where a water display on the local dam is a big thing to do on a Saturday afternoon.

I would zoom in on my skis and the boys would run up and pick up my skis and bring me my towel and even though I was like Esther Williams gone wrong, they didn't seem to mind that too much. I think they quite liked me.

In my glory days, those long ago days of my 'fifteen minutes of fame', I became a Springbok and the South African Women's Champion, and got to wear the 'green and gold', which had been a really big thing once. It was a big thing still when I did it, but not quite what it had once been because of what was happening politically in South Africa at that time.

It isn't easy to go into international competition when nobody likes what's happening back home in the country you happen to come from. In fact, it's very hard because you're there to ski. Anyone who's ever competed in any sport at international level will tell you what a long hard road it is to get there. All you really want to do is your best and maybe come back with a medal to show everyone's faith in you is justified and they haven't been wasting their time.

When you get the feeling that people are polite on the surface but shying away from you inside, it's hard not to take it personally and at a certain level it hurts. You know how people talk about collecting baggage as we make our way through life? When we left South Africa, without fully comprehending it, we were carrying all kinds of baggage along with us. So there were lots of questions about what was going on in our country and what we were doing about it besides skiing, and people were entitled to ask them; they were right to do so. The trouble was that we were young, we hadn't had much opportunity to look at our country from the outside before, and we really had no answers to give them.

I like to think most people liked us for ourselves, but they didn't make any bones about not liking what was going on back where we came from and the best we could do was to say that we didn't like it either.

Sometimes on the international circuit when people asked us where we came from we'd say Australia because their colours were the same as ours. It sounds very cowardly now but we did it because it was easier.

It isn't very nice to feel ashamed in the way we were ashamed and as I got older, I realised that dodging issues in this way is no solution, and I wasn't very proud of myself at all.

My father's father, my missionary grandfather, worked among the so-called coloured people of Beaufort West in the middle of nowhere in the Karoo. When my father was growing up there was a curfew for people who weren't white. A big bell rang at nine o'clock and all the coloured people had to leave the town for the night. You have to be a very indifferent kind of person to sleep comfortably in your bed when that bell reminds you each night what is happening in your own town and my father was never reconciled to any notion of 'separateness'. For him a human being was exactly that and as a doctor, concerned with physical wellbeing, I suppose he saw people often as simply the sum of their component physical parts. There was no space at all for colour or creed. He didn't mind removing pieces of a person or replacing them. I think it's given my daughter Karen a bit of an aversion to medicine.

My father liked Karen – perhaps because she's very direct and that's a quality he always liked in a person. He thought it might be nice if she studied medicine, but she said, 'Not a chance.' She didn't like the idea of 'digging into anybody's insides', which was just fine with me. We all use our skills the best way we can. My father used his skills to help anyone who needed it and I would like to think that in our different ways, all of our family are like that.

Maybe, if I'd been older and known more about life, I might have said in reply to the awkward questions that were put to me when we were touring Australia that there were people back home in South Africa who were brave and doing courageous things and sometimes the world hears about it and sometimes it doesn't.

As for me, I live my life out on a much smaller canvas, but I grew up in a house where the door was always open to anyone who chose to walk through it. It didn't matter what colour they happened to be. There was always enough in the pot to offer a plate of food. That was how our family lived then. It's how we live now.

Perhaps it's only a very small thing but it's the only way we know. We have accepted comfort and support when we've needed it and offered it, in our turn, when we've been able to do so. I know this doesn't make us in any way exceptional. I say it only because it is, always has been and always will be our way.

I don't for a minute think this would have sounded like much of an answer to some of our questioners out in Australia and in the grand scheme of things I don't suppose it really matters much. The fact is, though, that everything starts with the individual and if you begin with just one person of goodwill a great many things far beyond our imagining can be possible.

In any case, we were in Australia to ski and that's what we did and we did our best and for the record let it be said that in 1965, in Surfer's Paradise, Australia, I was ranked second in the world.

I suppose you can say that the Australian competition and

achieving such a high ranking were the high point of my water-skiing career. When I came home my parents were there to meet me.

This is how my father saw it. He wrote:

> Deirdre came running into the reception hall at the airport. She talked about everything except her achievements. I wanted to know about the competition and how well she'd done, but she only told her mother and me how wonderful Australia was and about the fascinating people she'd met there.

In a contribution to *Chris Barnard: By Those Who Know Him*, Sir Roy Calne, a distinguished colleague of my father, divided him up under five sub-headings (with a pen, happily, and not with a scalpel, which might have come more naturally to him): 'Barnard: A Man Hungry for the Top', 'Hard Work,' 'Daughter', 'Endeavour', and 'Death'.

Looking at it now I'm surprised 'Daughter' got a look in at all. In fact, the rest just about sums up all my father's life and could have saved a great many other writers, including my father himself, quite a lot of verbiage, never mind all the trees that are sacrificed to make just one book.

As 'Daughter' in this case was me, I admit to having taken some interest. It takes a bit of time and experience to learn that reading about yourself, especially someone else's opinion of you, is not necessarily the most constructive way to pass the time. In any case, I was young and I did decide to read what someone had written about me, and in the words of Sir Roy Calne this is 'me':

> The ambition of Barnard was well suited to his own abilities but could not be transferred to his daughter, despite the most intense psychological onslaught on the girl. She had a

natural talent for waterskiing and won several minor championships. She appeared to have the potential to win international fame as a waterskier but to quote from the book [my father's book, *One Life*] 'She did not have the killer instinct needed to become a world champion,' and, as Barnard said, 'I have failed to transplant into her my own hunger for victory. She was still not going to beat her fists and cry if she lost. She could laugh it off. She would never make it.

'She was just too damned nice. The time had come to cease using my daughter to satisfy my own ambitions.'

That's my father and that's me. These words didn't hit home at that moment. They didn't hit home for a very long time, and when they did, it came at some cost, but I know something now that I didn't know then. It's nice and tidy to be 'the best'. But it all depends what you in your heart want to be best at. I would like to be the best person I can be. I would like to be the best wife and mother. I would like to think I am and have been a good daughter.

Prof. Peter Jackson, a colleague of my father who had once, I think, liked him very much, expressed himself as being 'disillusioned later'. It's amazing how quickly people become 'disillusioned' with someone when he has the nerve to become famous and actually enjoy it. He also had something to say about me.

Before the 'great event' Chris had apparently only one ambition, which he pursued with the utmost ruthlessness and singlemindedness, namely to make his daughter the world champion waterskier. Maybe he would have succeeded, but the heart transplant came first and, after this, his daughter nowhere. I saw her from time to time – a charming girl but bewildered by the sudden turn of events.

It's all a question of point of view, isn't it? Is that me he's writing about? I think the 'nowhere' is rather harsh and I'm not sure it's quite true but there's something I do know. Prof. Jackson was a nice man, he meant well, but as far as I know, hiking up mountains was his 'thing' and by the way, waterskiing wasn't all bad. Had Prof. Jackson, I wonder, ever been out on the water on a really good day when all of your body tells you that you're skiing right on top of your form? I ask only because he seems to know such a very great deal about it.

Skiing was important in those days but you don't have to be a rocket scientist to work out that as far as waterskiing or anything is concerned, there's nothing wrong with being 'good enough'. That's more than enough for most people and it's certainly more than enough for me. Nevertheless, I did try.

4

How I got to Australia in the first place

The part no one tells you about.
That important part people forget when
they say, 'Now that's what I call talent.'
In other words – the hard work

The life of any athlete who competes at international level is not an easy one (ask Tiger Woods, ask poor, late Hansie Cronje, ask Serena Williams) and waterskiing is no exception.

People who know us know that we lived by the lake, Zeekoevlei, to make it easier for me to keep up with my training. It may seem strange to some people that a family would move an entire household just because they have a daughter who waterskis.

There were not many people skiing at that time. It was still a fairly exotic sport in South Africa. I suppose because first of all, you need to be near water, which is a bit hard if you live in the hinterland; and you need a boat.

People said there must be something wrong with my family. Later on, when we were a bit more in the public eye, there were apparently so many things wrong with us you couldn't even begin to count them, let alone keep track of what they all were. In those days what it meant was that we were the crazy family who moved out to Zeekoevlei just so 'the daughter' would be able to practise every day, but the Barnards are not people who do things by halves. I sometimes think it would have made life a lot easier if we had been, but the trouble is, we don't know how.

Actually, it wasn't all that crazy, even though it wasn't exactly convenient. It meant two buses and a train to and from school for my brother and me. It meant a drive to the hospital for my father when another suburb would have placed all of us just a spit away from where we needed to be. It meant there was no happily situated convenience store for my mother to shop at, entailing a fair-sized trek to the nearest supermarket, but that's the way it is if you want to be a competitor.

So there we were by our lake, Zeekoevlei, which in English of course is Hippopotamus Lake. It's a very pretty lake, although considering what came later in those days of my fat phase, it was perhaps not as fortunately named as it might have been.

Being a competitive waterskier at international level is hard work. It was hard work for me and hard work for my father too because he was my coach. We used to get up at six in the morning. At six on a winter morning, knowing you have to get up, tog up and get out on the water doesn't exactly make you want to bounce out of bed. You don't have a sudden surge of energy that makes you want to run around the place yelling for your gear, saying you just can't wait to get out there and start doing your thing.

You already know what it's like out there because you've been there before. It's freezing cold. You know that within the next ten minutes or so you're going to be soaking wet. Your coach, who is also your father, is going to be yelling back into the wind at you to tell you where you've gone wrong and to get you to do it just one more time until it looks something a bit closer to fairly respectable, if not quite perfect.

If you would like to know what crazy is, I will tell you. That is crazy, but I did it anyway.

I want to tell you what we wore for training in those days and when I've done that I want to tell you two things very few people know.

We didn't have 'gear' like today's 'gear'. The wet suits we wore in summer weren't enough to keep out the winter cold. So in winter we wore dry suits. I sometimes wonder if I am the last person left on the planet who actually knows what a dry suit is. I'll tell you because I believe it is a truly useful piece of anthropological information. Before long the only place you will see a dry suit is somewhere like the National Geographic Museum Explorers Hall in Washington DC, where such things are kept for posterity, and when you do, if anyone ever asks you, you can say Deirdre Barnard told you about it first.

You put a dry suit on over a tracksuit. The tracksuit is to keep you warm. The dry suit looks like one of those old diving suits the deep-sea divers used to wear. You look like a moon man and the suit weighs a lot. You get into it through a big hole in the chest, but of course a big hole in the chest was nothing new to my father. You climb in and then you have a round glass bubble screwed on the front to close up the hole, and as if that isn't enough, you get tied up with rubber tubing just to keep everything in place.

I am not talking modern times here but that's how it was in those days. It wasn't exactly the kind of thing to give a girl a taste for haute couture and it's amazing to think that someone who started out like that would ever know what a Pucci print or a Carrera pump was, but I did. I don't regularly swan around in such items myself, although when I babysat Barbara's sons I did once or twice try her shoes on just for the feel of them!

I have now reached the stage where comfortable is good. I don't turn up my nose at a nice pair of slimming black pants from Woolies and if they have an elasticised waistband that's good enough too, but I like nice things the same as anyone does and when the time came, I found I could learn.

As far as the dry suit goes, I just want to say, because it really can't matter to anyone now, that my being properly equipped was very important to my father. He liked things done right and so I had the best possible tubing to tie it all together, my father saw to that too. My tubing came from Groote Schuur Hospital and was used in the medical procedures there so you can be sure it was just about the best tubing you could get.

People have said to me I cannot put in a book the fact that my father 'helped himself' to this tubing, which actually belonged to the Provincial Administration, but I don't think it matters. My father is gone now, and I think it can hurt no one to know that he did help himself to the tubing. He did it in the old days, long before it was the fashion for people to steal everything they can lay their hands on in a hospital, and I suppose he did it in what he considered a good cause.

You can just imagine what I looked like. It was 'Michelin man, eat your heart out'. I suppose that in its way the suit did what it had to do but it really did look pretty bizarre and there's something else too. When you spend so much time in the water, you're forever getting water in your ears and your mother is forever having to take you to ENT specialists to try to get it out.

My Namibian grandparents were perhaps not as familiar with water as we were. In fact, rain and water in any quantity is a totally foreign concept to many children in Namibia because, very often, they have to wait a very long time before they actually see it with their own eyes.

My aunt Cora didn't see rain until she was eleven years old and she got such a fright seeing fat drops of water falling down from heaven that she went quite hysterical and nearly didn't make twelve. That's how things are there. Where my grandparents lived in Namibia, if they see rain once every five years they're lucky, never mind a whole lakeful every day of their lives. No wonder our life, as immersed in water as it was, seemed a little bit peculiar to them.

My grandfather did not think it fair that the buck on his farm, for example, had wonderful ears while his granddaughter's were permanently waterlogged. He thought the solution lay in the oil in a small gland you find in a buck's hoof.

Every hunting season we got a supply of the oil. It came in a little pod straight from the buck and went straight into my ears. It sounds weird and got weirder in the sense that I kept using it – it became a sort of ritual to bring me luck – but I suppose it did help. I think of those poor buck and really hope that their sacrifice was not in vain, but the truth is that I really can't remember. There was so much else I had to keep in my mind that there just wasn't any room for anything more.

I had to do trick skiing, slalom and ramp jumping. I hated trick skiing. Our boat in those days was called *Pacemaker*. Before that we'd had a boat called *Louwtjie* and my father used to put sandbags in the back of the boat to make the wakes bigger.

When my father looked back from behind the wheel to see how I was doing I'd show with a motion of my hand that the water was too choppy for me to do anything. He never bought this.

I used to get fed up with him.

'If you're so good at it why don't you do it yourself?' I'd yell.

'What then?' he'd call back. 'I do the skiing and you come and take over my operating theatre? I don't think so.'

Then he'd look ahead again and I'd start all over again except that this time I'd be crying out of frustration. You've heard about 'crying buckets', but have you ever heard of a lake made up entirely of tears? There were plenty of mornings when I believed what my mother said, that Zeekoevlei was made up completely of tears and all of them had been shed by me.

I look at young athletes on TV sometimes, so beautiful in their moment of glory, collecting their medals and accolades. I swell with pride for them, even though I don't know them. Being recognised and having a medal hung around your neck is a wonderful thing, but I can see something else too. I can see the sweat, the tears, that time clock ticking away and the way you put your own physical resources under pressure to see just how far you can go. Then there are those days you think you have no chance at all of ever making it. I know what deep-in-the-bone weariness is, that desperate kind of tiredness all competitive athletes face, knowing all the time that you can't give up. There's no such thing as 'give up'. The only thing there is, is the certainty that however hard you've worked, however tired you are, all that lies ahead of you is more of the same and harder work still.

Something people tend to forget is that my father was a gifted sportsman himself. He said himself that he was never a good spectator. Either he was playing the game or he just wasn't interested (and I think you could probably say the same for his life). Before his career and his life intervened he played any sport he was invited to join in on and he played it well.

At one time my father was team manager for the waterski team and at one time he was a judge. One year he was chairman of the ski committee, and during the time that the South African Waterski Championships were held at Zeekoevlei, he was responsible for the critical job of laying down the buoys.

There was a howling gale the day this had to be done. My father had to go out himself in his wetsuit and make quite sure everything was being done according to the rules laid down by the South African Waterskiing Association, and he was a man who took such things very seriously.

He and Harry Bloomberg, the national chairman, and Van, one of the young technicians from my father's laboratory, went out in *Pacemaker*. They had to make sure the buoys were adequately weighted with cement and then use a measuring rope to mark the exact position of each buoy.

It was the most terrible weather. Rain came pouring down, the wind howled and the water was very choppy. I kept thinking they'd give up, but they didn't. My mother sent me down to the jetty with a flask of hot coffee. I thought they'd come back then, but they didn't. They just drank it down and went straight back to the job of laying out the slalom course. I knew that to do something properly you had to have just that kind of focus and tenacity. That, I knew, was what my father was like, and I just stood on the end of the jetty and watched them.

I watched them until I realised how really cold and utterly miserable it was and then I went back into the house and left them to get on with the job. With hindsight, I realise that I probably took much of his effort for granted.

I think sometimes of my girl-self standing on that jetty alone in that awful weather, watching my father in the half-light, bent to his work in a boat bobbing within my vision but away from the shore.

My father was a very determined man. He had a great ability to focus totally on the task at hand. I realised in that moment that he was oblivious to everything and everyone around him, including me. I could see him, I could have called out to him if I had wanted to. Yet he was removed from me and I was suddenly very conscious of the fact that although he was my father, we inhabited totally different spaces. It was a quick flick of memory's shutter, a 'snapshot' of a winter morning, that's all. Yet I wonder if, in some way, the future had not already begun to move towards me and if I had not, in fact, intuited far more than I actually saw.

Growing up Calvinist

... and the Calvin we're talking
about here is not Calvin Klein

In those days, when I was the doctor's daughter and lived with my parents in the house by the lake at Zeekoevlei, I had no idea at all how my life would turn out. I expected, hopefully, to grow up, finish school, go to university and maybe do something useful with my life. My parents were keen on 'useful'. I come from a long line of people who are raised with the idea that their life is there for them to do useful things with, people who would find it slightly embarrassing if someone in their own family turned out any other way. The bright lights are not for people like us. At least, this is the official line. My grandfather on one side was a clergyman and on the other, a farmer. My father's mother believed that dancing was the quickest way to Hell.

This is not the kind of stock that produces daughters who find themselves on the front page of the tabloids or the back page of the *Sunday Times*, but I can see now from my own experience that life can push you in any direction it likes. It can give you a hard time or it can make you a star. I'm not really all that certain that you have very much say in the matter.

No one expected my father to be famous. He certainly didn't. When it happens to you it's really very strange. People who would normally walk right past you without noticing you on the street suddenly stop and take notice. If you are the child of such a person, there you are, caught in the glow from the halo. Suddenly, just because you happen to be there, you appear to have curiosity value, and it isn't always easy.

People you don't know come over and ask you questions. In fact, people ask the kinds of questions they'd probably think twice about asking people they know far better than they'll ever know you, and sometimes it made me wish I hadn't been brought up the way I had. You see, my mother always said to be courteous and friendly and always answer questions as truthfully and politely as you can. My mother knows how to raise children and there was a time I used to be all in favour of the kind of upbringing I had, but now I'm not so sure.

There can be a lot of problems that go with this particular territory and some day, if they haven't already, someone will write a handbook called *Calvinist Guilt: Ten Ways to Handle It* and I'll be the first one in the bookshop to buy it. There have been times in my life when I could have done with some help. As in, quite a large helping of help, actually.

A lot of the questions I'm asked have to do with my father. First of all, there's my father and my mother. It's hardly a secret that my father and mother divorced, but even so, especially at the time the divorce was happening, how I felt about it was a question that kept coming up. I would have thought the answer was fairly obvious and that it was hardly worth the trouble of singling me out to ask how I felt about it. There are far too many children who have stood by and watched while their parents divorced, knowing all the time in their hearts that they had no power at all to do anything to stop it.

Divorce, no matter who's doing the divorcing and who gets caught in the middle, is not a happy story. Any child from a divorced home could tell you about that if you asked them, and when you're one of the children involved all you'll be able to say when you get right down to it is that there wasn't very much you could do.

Divorce comes and goes, and it goes the way of all nine days' wonders. It gets smaller and smaller until no one is really all that interested in it any more, because all that remains is the fact that it's a reality. It's over and done and it's history.

Unless you happen to be directly involved, in which case (in my case) there were always the questions about My Father and the 'Wives'; My father and his 'Friends'; My Father: His Role in My Weight Gains and Weight Losses – that kind of thing.

If I told you the kinds of questions people have asked me about my father over the years you would fall flat on your back, but I decided long ago that it was all right. Do you remember Annette Bening in *American Beauty*? How she plays the part of an estate agent and the scene where she's all by herself inside a house she simply must sell and keeps saying out loud all the time, 'I can do this!' while actually she's holding onto herself so she doesn't fall to pieces? That was how I was. That's how hard it was to answer those questions.

I could have let it upset me and sometimes it did. I could have let it bother me and sometimes it did that too, but in the end I decided the old ways were best and I might just as well do what my parents taught me and be as polite and as helpful as I could. After all, it didn't take too long after my father made his first headline before I began to learn that for a very great deal of the rest of my life this was likely to go with the territory. Sometimes the territory is not very much to one's liking.

For all of his 'famous' life my father's comings and goings were of great interest to the press and in the nature of things, sometimes that interest was generous and genuine. More often, though, it was simply probing and prurient. Once he became a public figure there was no 'no-go' zone, no private place in my father's life.

I read somewhere something that stays with me. 'We tolerate a level of intrusion into people's private lives which makes journalists barely distinguishable from stalkers.' I have had some experience of this and it makes me sad.

It's an interesting thing that goes on between journalists – who surely, to be unbiased, must have scepticism as a tool of their trade – and those people they solicit interviews from. Interviewees, of course, very often yield themselves up more than willingly. Some are vain, some are ignorant and some, I suppose, are just glad of the attention.

First there's the flattery and seduction and then, in the interests of a good story, must come the betrayal. It seems as if it can only very rarely be any other way.

Rather a sad liaison, then, forms as a result of all this wooing by the media. As any parent might warn a child bent on irresponsibility, it can only end badly.

In my father's case there was also a careful cataloguing of the gradual loss of the much-spoken-of 'good looks' of his youth.

Good looks, we all know, don't last forever, and we all know that the great French moralist was right when he said, 'In the misfortunes of our best friends, we find something that is not unpleasing.' You can double the enjoyment when the person in question is not exactly a friend and happens to be famous. There's a kind of perverse interest in someone once beautiful who loses those looks everyone once had so much to say about, and the media love it. Once someone who was once beautiful has passed their peak they can't wait to find the absolutely worst photograph they possibly can, and this is the one they'll publish.

Same goes for fatness. Try *Hello* magazine or any of its siblings.

Is Madonna pregnant or just overweight? And Kate Winslet? Weight gain is big news and so is weight loss, just ask Kate Moss.

Why, someone asked me, are you so good-humoured about your own yo-yo weight problems and so protective about your father and the loss of his much-vaunted looks?

The answer is simple. You can control your weight. You can do very little about getting old. You may rage against it – my father certainly did – but in the end he found no antidote for it. He became old just as we all do – and because he was a man whose powers were waning, who could do nothing at all while all that he once had been slowly began ebbing away, leaving him vulnerable and somehow exposed – I felt protective towards him.

In his last years my father was not physically well. His old bugbear, arthritis, plagued him. It had been his constant companion since the long ago days in Minneapolis in the fifties when it had first been diagnosed. His first intimation that something was seriously wrong had come on one of those most innocent of days, the way these life-changing things often do.

As a treat, we were having a family outing. Andre and I were to be taken out ice-skating and that was a big thrill for us.

The cold in its way is very beautiful. Keeping steady on your skates on the ice is quite an achievement. Skating is a wonderful occupation for children, round as balls, upholstered in layer upon layer of warm winter clothing. I loved it. I loved making heat hazes with my breath on the icy air. I loved being together as a family, with my parents laughing and urging us on. I loved the cold weather and all the people bundled up in winter clothes just like we were, with hats pulled down over their ears and ear muffs and the air so thin, it hurt just to breathe it. I loved the freedom of the ice, the way you can glide across it with your hands in bright gloves free for waving. I was perfectly happy in that way that you sometimes can be.

Ice-skating is a pretty chilly occupation. We all felt cold, particularly our feet, but life was changing even though we couldn't know it. My father felt the coldness as a deep and persistent ache that wouldn't go away. He sought medical advice. The diagnosis was rheumatoid arthritis.

The news was absolutely devastating to him. He was a doctor and knew the implications. He knew the impact the disease would have on his career, which was burgeoning at that time. He knew the prognosis for rheumatoid arthritis because he'd come across cases himself during the course of his career. It is not hard to imagine that every worst-case scenario he could envisage played itself through his mind as the full impact of what was happening to him began to sink in.

He was extremely lucky. It may sound strange to you that I say this, but he said so himself. Not because such a painful and crippling disease had been visited upon him, but because of the way his colleague, the diagnostician in Minneapolis, talked with him about it. He discussed the different forms of the disease. He pointed out to my father that although there was no way the diagnosis – which was pretty frightening in itself, especially for a surgeon – could be wished away, there were nevertheless positive aspects that should be considered. It was not arthritis in its most virulent form. That it would handicap him was inevitable, but the nature of the particular form he was suffering from was such that it wouldn't end with him totally withered, confined to a wheelchair, his quality of life totally destroyed.

'He gave me hope.' That is what my father said afterwards. 'Nothing is more important than that.'

It was something he tried to do with his own patients even more vigorously after he'd been a patient himself. It was something he incorporated into his own attitude to life, something he passed on to his children. No matter how bad things seem to be, there is always the undeniable possibility that eventually they will improve. To abandon hope just doesn't make sense.

Jewish people have a proverb: 'To abandon hope is to insult the future.' My father would never have done that. He was a man who saw possibilities in even the most daunting medical prognosis, and outside the medical environment, he was a man who was positive about life. He was always excited about what the future might hold and he was particularly enthralled by the progress being made in his own field and those fields adjacent to it, and liked to keep himself up to date.

My father's arthritis was to plague him for the rest of his life and so was his asthma. In later life he had a hip replacement and there was the terrible disfiguring skin cancer that affected his nose. I nagged him to have it attended to.

I said he looked like the Elephant Man. Perhaps you think that's a terrible thing to say, but everyone knows doctors are the worst patients. He kept putting off having it attended to.

One of my problems is that I can't keep my mouth shut even when I know I've gone on about something far too long already. The other problem, which is just as bad and probably even worse, is that I don't always think before I speak and it often lands me in trouble.

My father took the Elephant Man remark with good grace. At least it made him, in his own way, address the issue. He dipped his face in friar's balsam and came out a very funny colour but in the end it didn't help at all, just as he knew it wouldn't. He had to have the nose problem professionally attended to.

I don't know if you know how this is done but it goes something like this. A skin growth to produce a flap of 'spare' skin is encouraged on the forehead. When the operation takes place and the cancerous areas are removed from the nose, the nose itself is rebuilt out of this specially grown skin and the forehead goes back to being its normal self again.

In my father's case, I think the cancer went deeper than the doctors originally thought. The spare skin they'd grown for the operation proved insufficient and some extra skin had to be taken from the sides of his cheeks.

I'm sorry if this isn't for the squeamish, but they'll just have to bite the bullet and remember that it's a lot easier to read about this than to actually have it done to you.

The end result was, in my father's opinion, that this was just about the best facelift anyone could have asked for. (And whether we like it or not, my father's opinion was very much sought after by certain people in his day, and on the matter of facelifts, as well as quite a few other things.) His forehead was now smooth and flat. His cheeks were pulled tight forward. The only problem was that his ears, which after The Feet (see Chapter 8) were not what anyone could consider his best feature, came right along with his cheeks. They sat further forward than they ever had before but there was nothing he could do about that.

He said he was the only person he knew who, if he wanted to present himself properly, had to shave his ears when he shaved the rest of his face in the morning because they were pulled so far forward.

I think there are things we all know without having them spelled out for us. Getting older is not all it's cracked up to be. It's nice to talk about 'autumn years' or 'the prime of life'. It's not so nice if you happen to be the person who's slowly starting to go to pieces.

There's not very much any of us can do about it. In my father's case the list of things going slowly wrong was just as long as and probably longer than a great many other people's. I'm quite sure he was aware of it. If he hadn't been, there was always a journalist to remind him.

In this case, a gentleman called William Sanderson-Meyer, a contributor to the *Saturday Argus* who had a column called 'Jaundiced Eye'. On 25/26 August 2001, four or five days before my father died, he wrote about 'Passing your sell-by date'. Of my father he wrote:

Last week I saw pictures in the newspaper of a seedy look-ing fellow with a few thin strands of lank hair plastered in neat agricultural rows across his balding head.

His lumpy, large nose looked as if a dyslexic kindergarten pupil had put it together out of play dough. He had mottled skin and haunted eyes.

It was only when I read the caption that I found out that it was the world famous heart surgeon and one-time play-mate of the Hollywood stars, Dr Christiaan Barnard, who was commenting on some new research in combating heart disease.

It was horrific.

This was the last article in a South African publication to make reference to my father before his death.

I have always felt a great tenderness towards those who are vul-nerable: the aged, small children, the abused, the powerless. I have truly felt in my heart a great surge of feeling toward them. This has been one of the major forces that have governed my life and I don't necessarily recommend it as a way to chart one's life course. I can almost understand why some people steel themselves and pull away from it. Sometimes I've sat still for a while and looked at the world and felt sad and helpless and powerless in myself to do any-thing that would make a meaningful difference, but there's some-thing else too and there's some comfort that: at the heart of it, feeling kinship with some other person, understanding their pain and being willing to take some part of it onto oneself, is what makes us human.

I have known some sad things in my life. I have known loss and pain. I've seen them up close. I know what it is to be sad and I've cried my share of tears, but I see now that there's another place too, and a different kind of hurt, one that takes one beyond tears. I had not myself been confronted by wilful and self-indulgent cruelty before. I did not know it then but I know it now.

~

You would think there would be an end to it and that after my father died the interest that surrounded him would ebb, but that isn't so. There are still media people on the telephone and the e-mail. There are two biographies I know of currently in preparation. You would think people would have asked everything they wanted while he was still here with us and they could ask him themselves, but it isn't like that either. There are still people who have questions.

'I am "doing" a piece on Chris Barnard,' they say. 'I was wondering if you could perhaps help me?'

Janet Malcolm, herself a rather controversial biographer, has an interesting view of this craft. 'Biography is the medium through which the remaining secrets of the famous dead are taken from them and dumped out in full view of the world.' That's what she writes and she's right. Still, I try to help, which probably says more about me than it does about potential biographers. Sometimes I have the answers and sometimes I don't. Then there are those times when I'm unpacking my life for the hundred and twenty-five millionth time so that some or other researcher (recommended, with good intentions, credentials impeccable) can rake through it again in the hope that maybe they can find something about my father everyone else has missed.

There's something infinitely sad about this. When my father died that essence that made him the man he was died too. There are no letters, diaries or stories recounted that can even begin to capture the tiniest part of all those energies that surge together and make a human being quite unique and different from their fellows.

That is what the sadness of death is really all about. That unique spark is gone and the fragile essence that makes up the person can never be recounted or recaptured no matter how hard we try. That is the pity of it.

Life with Father

'Well, that's Dad.'
[Me, 1987]

When I started writing this book I was thinking that if what I put down ever grew into a book I would call it *Love & Pain & the Whole Damn Thing*. I would have liked that, but that title's already taken. I liked it because it's true and it's true not just for me. There can't be a single person who's ever lived any kind of life who couldn't look at that title, hang their own life story underneath it and find out that it looks as if it belongs there. The same goes for me.

When my father was no longer young, when his marriage to Karin had come to its end and he'd set up home on his own again, I'd go with him when he went swimming in the pool in the town-house complex where he lived.

It was quite a caravan. There was my father in his bath-robe and me behind, talking, carrying the towel and a book and looking for the keys so we wouldn't get locked out, while he worked through the checklist. Did I have the towel? Did I remember to bring the keys, and what about the asthma pump? I would have to show him I had it just so that he could be sure. Through the garden we would go, past the gardeners, with me talking and doing the 'hullo, hullo' thing (see Chapter 9) to anyone who happened to be there, and looking for a nice spot where my father could spread his things out and I could set out a 'chaise' so that he could be comfortable, while the blue pool blinked in the sun and the Kreepy-Krauly sucked its way around.

After his swim it would be the same thing all over again. My father would go into the sauna, I'd go into the sauna with him and I'd read to him.

One of the books I read him was *Angela's Ashes* by Frank McCourt and out of that book slid a sentence written by Mr McCourt, read by me and heard by my father. 'Children love their parents unconditionally.' That's what it said. It never said if this was wise or advisable or even if it was comfortable. If you asked me I would tell you that it's none of those things. People talk casually about 'unconditional love'. What they don't tell you is – if you find yourself having embraced it – just how much it can hurt. There are plenty of parents out there who can tell you this and plenty of children too.

My father and I didn't discuss it at length but it occurred to us both that in its way this was rather a sad thought. It might not have been significant to him but it stayed with me. I never lay awake at night thinking about why that one statement fixed itself in my head the way it did. Yet as I read it, something inside me just responded to it. I thought, 'Yes, and that's all right too. That's how it's been for me and that's how it should be.'

I used to try slipping my father self-help books as well but he never bought into that. He told me he knew what I was up to and if I didn't mind, he'd prefer it if I skipped 'all that psychological stuff'.

I came into my father's life when he was 28 years old. He was 78 when he died. No matter which way you look at it, 50 years is a long time to know someone.

It actually feels quite funny to write down the words 'my father'. I have a picture in my head of people who have read this far and have been waiting for 'the second shoe to drop', wondering how long it will be before I really get into the business of my father. Now here we come to it, they'll say. I'm not sure that they're going to find what they're looking for within these pages.

It was something, though. Having a father like mine did make my life a little bit different. Whether we like it or not, whether we wish it or would prefer it otherwise, the people closest to us do have a hand in determining the way our life goes.

If you asked me I would say I was happy being 'the doctor's daughter' and living out at Zeekoevlei. If it had stayed that way our lives would still have had their ups and downs, but they would have been different.

As it turned out, a funny kind of spotlight fell on me and my family and it ended up with me going along that road first Robert Frost and then F Scott Peck called 'the road less travelled'. Sometimes I liked it and sometimes it wasn't all that great, but isn't that life, after all? Isn't that your life and your friend's; or the life of the woman standing behind you in the food market at Woolies if only you could pluck up the courage to ask her?

Sometimes I drive along Beach Road in Sea Point right near the SABC and there's a woman who stands at the traffic light selling *The Big Issue* and sporting an HIV Positive T-shirt. The ladies who sunbathe their days away come down to display themselves, the mothers wait at the crossing with their children, joggers run past and the dog walkers too, although their pace is different.

Who pays any real attention to her?

The fancy cars come and go. They pull up at the red light, these people who must seem to her to have everything their hearts could desire, but none of them has a smile as big as hers or an attitude as generous. She's proud of her job and she earns her bread. She's right to be proud. She has achieved something. She's someone.

Some people ignore her but there are a great many more who know who she is and look out for her. She is someone in her own right and something's for sure, she also has a story to tell.

What I would like is to come to the end of my life and be glad that this has been my life; to feel that I found it worth living and would gladly live it again if I were offered the chance.

It's strange to think that, after all this time, my father has come to the end of his journey while my life goes on. It makes me think of all those questions people have asked me over the years, the genuinely interested ones and those others who were just digging around looking for something to gossip about.

I thought about the waterskiing, the divorces, his wives, my stepmothers, and what it feels like when people ask you if you don't mind it when your parents' private affairs are all over the newspapers.

It can hardly come as a great revelation if I say that of course I minded. As it happened, I minded rather a lot, but there wasn't very much I could do about it.

I think about how total strangers have stood looking at me, waiting for me to come out with an answer, when I have really had no words adequate to express how I feel.

People ask me if I wasn't angry about what happened in my family, and the answer is that, yes, of course I was. I was very angry indeed, but I wasn't so stupid that I was going to keep beating my head against a wall, railing against things that can't be changed. My world, the world I now found myself in, which was not my perfect world, was not going to change. Any change that took place now would have to come from me.

I went to a psychiatrist. I talked a lot and yes, I talked about my parents, the divorce and all those things that were written in the newspapers. I talked about all our private family business being hung out for everyone to see. As if someone had come into our house, rifled through all our most private things, picked on what they thought was the juiciest stuff and gone off, gleefully and triumphantly, carrying their loot with them.

I poured out my life to the psychiatrist and I poured out my pain. I have opinions about 'voicelessness', the voicelessness of children, and elsewhere in this book I speak about how sometimes, especially where it concerns people you love, being silent and keeping your point of view to yourself is the best and most loving thing to do. But there is, I see now, another kind of voicelessness too and that is the inability to talk back when the media spotlight casts its distorting glare on the people you love most in the world. That is a terrible voicelessness and I found myself quite defenceless against it.

It is good to talk and it made a very pleasant change to have someone who listened and understood as the psychiatrist did, but talking and listening – getting a nice cleansing brainwash, if you like to put it that way – is not going to do the trick all by itself. Being angry isn't going to get you anywhere. You can't stay still and wallow in anger, no matter how tempting that may sometimes appear to be. You have to let it go. Easy to write down, not so easy to do, and yet it can be done and it's important that it should be done.

Look around you. Don't you know people so filled with anger at what they perceive as something being taken away from them that they can't think or talk about anything else? We all know someone like that, and where does it lead? Short answer: nowhere fast. It sits there and corrodes away into bitterness while the world moves on.

If you had a cancer growing inside you, you'd seek the help of an oncologist and do all you could to rid yourself of it. Anger's not any different from that. It stands in the way of your moving forward, and there's something else too. It's a very effective barrier against new relationships.

I love my mother. I don't tell her that nearly often enough. In fact, I think my mother is an exceptional woman and quite certainly the best mother anyone could possibly wish for. I have said that in all our turbulence she was always a safe haven, and she has been and is.

At one point, I needed to make peace with my mother. I telephoned her and in a clear and honest way told her all of my feelings and asked her forgiveness, because in my headstrong way I had blundered on with not enough consideration for how she might be feeling. I had not valued her nearly as highly as she deserved.

Such things have to be articulated. We all need to do this sometime and just hope that our doing what needs to be done gets the forgiving response that we hope for (as it did in my case), so we can go on with our lives. Yet, even if an overture is rejected once we have made it and we haved owned up to a fault, we have still cleared a way. We can still move on.

I have done self-improvement courses as well. Not because I think some outside force will suddenly fill the room and help me cope with my life better, but because I am a practical person. I know I need help to cope with certain things in my life and I gladly accept any tools that can help me.

One such course is the Landmark Forum. This has helped me a great deal. It has to do with crossroads in life. The 'What if this had happened'/'What if this had not happened' syndrome, if you like to call it that.

It helps you discover something quite wonderful which is right there looking at us all the time. In between all the 'What ifs' is the 'What is', what's happening right now in this moment. If we can just find that place and make it the best place we can, then, perhaps, we will have found the way to use our time fruitfully and not waste it by continually looking back at what has happened or anticipating that in a future, not yet arrived, things will be different.

So, yes, I've had people come up to me and ask me all kinds of things about my life and the goings on in my family and I have been deeply hurt and felt very vulnerable, which is not, trust me, the best way in the world to feel. But I think too about the funny times and what it feels like to have been the first and eldest child, the senior child in the Barnard family.

I may be self-appointed and self-titled but that's how I see myself. Sometimes the others say I'm the BBC, which is to say the Barnard Broadcasting Corporation, and I'm almost certainly that too, but I am the eldest. I was the first on the scene. If I'd fitted in somewhere else, I suppose that would have been different too.

I sometimes think about my father and about that poor king in *The King and I* with all of his family. I think my father was a bit like that in the end, especially if you count the grandchildren as well. There's a standing joke in our family that we don't have a family tree so much as a creeping vine and in fact, that's more or less the way it is.

The Full Catastrophe. That's what my father called us and that's what we were, and no one would have cared less about us or about any of it, except for a single four-letter word. (Please read on …)

Fame

'And then we told them who we were.'
'And who were you?'
[Anon]

I have a well-known father. It's no good pretending I haven't. I can hardly help knowing this and I may just as well say it and get it over with and out of the way once and for all.

Having someone famous in your family isn't the easiest thing in the world to ignore. You can't make it go away by pretending you'll wake up one morning and find it has disappeared in the night and everything has gone back to being just the same as it once was.

My father was no longer the young medical student who used to travel home by train in the holidays to see his family, knowing before he got there that the first thing he'd see was their high expectations of him just shining out of their eyes. After all, they were spending money they could ill afford on his training, hoping that in the future it would not turn out to be money wasted.

In those days he often travelled with another Beaufort West medical student called Percy Helman. Before the train pulled into Beaufort West station, where Percy's parents were also waiting for him, Percy used to pull out a bottle of ether and dab it all over himself like perfume.

'My mother has to smell that I'm studying to be a doctor,' he used to explain.

In the days of his fame my father didn't need to go around in a haze of ether for people to know what his job was.

What happens about fame is this. It attaches itself to a person's life, a little bit like a computer virus does. Then it just hangs round and every now and then, and usually when you least expect it, it gives you a shove that makes you remember it.

It isn't just that in *Clinical Cardiology: A Peer-Reviewed Journal for Advances in Cardiovascular Disease* one of my father's peers called him 'simply the most unforgettable character of the second generation of cardiac surgeons'. That counts for something in the medical profession. For me it was different. I'll give you just one example.

In those early days of my father's fame I was invited to be on a TV show in Stuttgart, Germany, and the show was called *I Carry a Famous Name*. Before you go on such a show you have, somewhere inside yourself, to agree that it's true – that you do carry a famous name. It's a small thing when you look at it like that. It's very different when it happens to you.

It's not like the slimming competition where you think you'd like the car, you'd love the trip on the *Oriana* and you really want to see Hollywood and have a chance of a screen test and everything. As far as that's concerned, you can take your prizes, meet a few new people, have a nice time and go home again. Carrying a 'famous name' is not so easy.

Once upon a time I had my own kind of fame with my water-skiing but it was quite a long time ago and I don't suppose there are many people around who remember it. It's like when you go to a party and someone pushes you forward as if people should know you, but you're not so sure they will, so you quickly say who you are before they take a guess and guess wrong. We all know how this feels, and no one wants anyone to be embarrassed.

I agree with what Andy Warhol said about everyone having fifteen minutes of fame, and there's something else too. Fame is not what it used to be. If they really want to, anyone can be famous these days. You don't have to work nearly so hard for it as you once did.

A lot of people are famous for very funny things. You can be famous for baking cakes. Marianne Faithfull wrote a whole book about it and she probably asked Martha Stewart to give her an endorsement for the way that she iced them, because Martha Stewart is famous for being able to do just this kind of thing – although Martha too has recently discovered something about fame: when it's good, it's very good, but when it's bad, it's horrid.

You can be famous just for knowing how to cut the hair of someone even more famous than you are. You can be famous even for spending your time hanging around someone famous. Paula Yates did. She did other things in her life too but in the end, when she died, that's all anyone seemed to want to remember her for.

You can be famous like Hansie Cronje, although that is a hard way to be famous and I don't really recommend it.

One day everybody loves you. You make them feel good and they can't do enough for you. Then something goes wrong. Nobody loves you anymore except when you die. Then it's all right to say that maybe there was a time once when you weren't so bad after all.

I have seen fame – the good side and the bad – and if you want my honest opinion I really don't think it's anything like it's cracked up to be, and this is not sour grapes, by the way. I have had my own soggy five minutes and they were nice while they lasted and that was quite enough for me.

People ask me if I am going to say anything in my book (in 'that book you're supposed to be writing' is what they actually say) about some of the famous women my father knew. I don't think so. First of all, for the really very old-fashioned reason that it actually is none of my business. Second, because some years ago I read a magazine article that gave a little formula for helping to understand parents and survive in one piece all the unpredictable things they might do. I no longer have that article, but this is the gist of it, with my own ideas added in. If these pointers can help you as they have me, you're welcome to them.

1. Realise that your parents are simply fallible people who make mistakes just like everyone else.
2. You are only one part of your parents' life. You don't know everything about them.
3. There's nothing wrong with being angry with a parent.
4. When a parent does something you don't like that hurts you, remember this is only one part of your relationship with them.
5. Your parents' problems belong to them …
6. … so you are not responsible for putting things right or sorting them out.

So? Answers to questions about my father's private life? See above, and the answer is really, what on earth for? All those glamorous women are pretty ancient by now. Some of them, sadly, are already dead, and the ones who are still with us are either face-lifted to the eyeballs, wear sunglasses so big you couldn't see what they looked like no matter how hard you tried, or don't go out in public any more.

That's how it is with glamour. That's how it is with glory. What's there to say except that no one stays young and beautiful forever? The old generation passes to make way for the new and all I can say is that I hope they had fun while their juices were running and I hope they think it was worth it.

The way my father told it, Sophia Loren at least had a life motto that makes me think she was a sensible woman with the right tools to take life on and make a success of it. Sophia had grown up poor and knew that people were more important than things.

Once, in New York, her hotel suite was broken into. The burglars threatened to kill her children if she didn't hand over her jewellery. Needless to say, the jewellery went, Sophia lived to tell the tale and the kids are alive and well and all grown up now. 'Never cry over things that can't cry over you,' was her life motto, she said.

I agree. In fact, it's easy for me to agree. I am not over-burdened with worldly goods, which is the way I prefer it, and my 'jewellery' wouldn't get anyone very far. People are far more important to me than things. In any case, I'm sure Sophia was sensible enough to have all those things not worth crying over fully insured. At least, I would hope so!

8

Being beautiful

'Vanity's a deadly sin.' [cf. Growing up Calvinist]
'If you've got it, baby, flaunt it.' [Mae West]
*'What's so bad about feeling good
about yourself?'* [Me]

Young people are beautiful. So are the very old. I see now, looking back, that even I – when I was young, in those days when I was doing the Fat Thing, before I became Mej. Viets – *het glad nie te bad gelyk nie*: I didn't look too bad at all. I wish I'd known it then, but *nou maar, toemaar* – that's life.

People say my father was a vain man. Perhaps he was. Now, when I look at photographs of him as a young man, it strikes me that perhaps my father had a certain 'something' and so who knows, he might very well have had something to be vain about after all?

Being born nice to look at is not for sissies. People expect you to go on being like that for the rest of your life. They feel cheated if you don't and even if you do the best job you can, it isn't ever really good enough.

How you look, how I look, is not a big issue. We have our bad hair days and it doesn't make the newspapers. Julia Roberts goes out looking like hell and the paparazzi are out there waiting to snap her and the newswires of the world are in business.

Brigitte Bardot – sun-raddled, riddled with arthritis and criss-crossed with lines – can love all the animals in the world just as much as she likes. She can raise as much funding as you can ever imagine to protect them, but when people see her picture they pounce on it and say, 'Now, isn't that a shame? She was so beautiful in her day.' The same goes for Elizabeth Taylor.

It's sad, but it's true. Life's like that. People seem somehow to be programmed to respond the way they do to situations like this, and it's a pity. Perhaps it's in the DNA. I don't know.

My daughter, Karen, has done some modelling. My half-brother Christiaan did some modelling too before he grew out of it. Come to think of it, our family have had more than our fair share of pictures in the glossies. My daughter wasn't the first Barnard who'd been on a magazine cover and there's no knowing whether she'll be the last. My father thought it was all well and good as far as it went. A nice sideline, perhaps, but not the way one should earn one's living. It was his view that while it is very nice to be beautiful enough to be a model, being beautiful is simply a bonus in life. It's lovely if you have it, it's there for us all to enjoy, but it isn't enough all by itself. When you are put on this planet a little bit more is expected of you than that. So in the light of this, it seems a bit funny that at the Versace for Africa fashion show in Cape Town in aid of the Mandela Children's Fund – Kate Moss, Naomi Campbell and Christy Turlington were there – three of the four local models chosen to strut the catwalk were Barnards. My Karen, was one of them. (But she's making shoes now and that's more practical employment.) Adam, the son of my late brother Andre and his wife Gail, did his bit too, and so did Christiaan. Probably too many Barnards again, but at least it was for a good cause.

People tend to like to look good. If they didn't, Estée Lauder and Elizabeth Arden and Nicky Clarke, as well as the entire Armani empire and goodness knows who else, could shut up shop and go right back where they came from.

One way or another our family have been much photographed and it's hard to talk about them without talking about looks. It would be polite not to mention this, but since over the years others have kept mentioning it, I thought I would throw it in for good measure.

My father's wife Barbara was a very beautiful woman. The famous photographer Patrick Lichfield thought so too. He said she was one of the most beautiful women in the world, and he should know, since there are very few beautiful people he hasn't met or photographed. What he said about Barbara is not just a very big compliment, although it's that too. It's really just the truth, no more and no less than that.

Patrick Lichfield is the Queen of England's cousin and he has photographed plenty of English 'Royals' in his time. I will not name names but I will say that you can give him a really plain girl and he can make her look like a film star. I don't know how he does it, but he does.

The big thing about Barbara is that she didn't need any tricks or anything funny done with lenses. She was just plain beautiful and that was that and anyone who knew her would agree with what Lichfield said. The first time I saw her I thought Barbara was the most beautiful girl I'd ever seen. I didn't even know her and I didn't know that I would soon find myself in such good company, having the Queen's cousin to share my opinion of her beauty.

The day Barbara came to Groote Schuur Hospital to 'introduce' herself to me while I was on my abortive weight-loss programme – but couldn't bring herself to go through with it – she was something to see.

I was happy enough there, but hospitals can be pretty monotonous places to be stuck in and it isn't every day someone like Barbara walks into a ward.

It was a bit like watching Wimbledon. You could just feel the heads swivelling. It wasn't only that she was terribly slim and wonderful to look at. She was also beautifully dressed, which I'll tell you about when we get to the part about My Life in the Rag Trade (which, incidentally, I would never have been launched into without help and encouragement from Barbara).

She had a look that I considered 'Continental', which was a look – with no disrespect to local is lekker – that definitely did not have 'Made in South Africa' stamped all over it. (I know we are all meant to buy Proudly South African now and help create jobs because Ruda Landman says so on television, but that was in those days and you didn't see someone dressed like that every day.)

On that day I was there in my pyjamas, probably with those telltale stains of illicitly obtained chocolate all over my mouth. And a ward in Groote Schuur Hospital is not exactly like the main lounge of the Mount Nelson Hotel when it comes to glamour.

What I saw was a tall beautiful girl more or less my own age in a very plain dress, all pinks and purples, who looked as if she'd walked straight off the cover of *Vogue*. I could see at once she'd come to the wrong place and I almost felt like going over to ask if I could help her.

Hospitals tend to be plain places. Barbara stood out for her radiance even when she was at a gala occasion. Against that rather utilitarian background she really did look like some gorgeous creature who had just dropped in from another planet.

She looked a bit uncertain in that way that someone who doesn't quite belong always does. She was there for a moment and then she was gone. I didn't realise that she'd been sent to find me, that my father had said in that easygoing way he had that as they were in a serious relationship and wanting to marry, she might go along an introduce herself to 'the daughter'. She did as he asked, but when the moment came she couldn't go through with it. I have never had stepchildren myself, but I suppose that if you're going to marry someone with children, meeting 'the daughter' for the first time can be a bit daunting.

She got cold feet. I think it was probably better that way. It would have been an awkward way for us to meet, although we would have made the best of it, but I'm glad I didn't meet her on that day or in that way. I still had my first radiant image of her and when I think of her now, that is how I like to remember her.

I suppose you might say that it was a bit unfair, to both of us, for my father to send Barbara to meet me in this way. I imagine that she could have said no and asked for a more structured kind of meeting, but she didn't. I expect she was in love and anxious to please, and of course I didn't have any say in the matter, but I didn't mind.

It's funny to think back to that time, but perhaps my father was a bit nervous. People talk about the 'younger wives' now but Barbara was the first 'younger wife' and everything was new then and perhaps he was a bit awkward about it. In any event, if he thought he'd bring the two of us together and leave us to sort it out, then that's what we eventually did, although not on that day.

Someone once asked me if the fact that Barbara was slim and I was – well – not so slim was an 'issue' between us. It wasn't. On a broader level, fat girls tend to envy thin girls and the world we live in makes thinness the ideal and seems to go out of its way to stoke up this envy, but fatness and friendship are two different things. The one shouldn't stand in the way of the other.

Barbara was lovely and she was, as I say, very beautiful and very willowy, but thin girls have their problems as well. They are under pressure to stay thin and keep in good shape and people get in their digs at them as well. 'Painfully thin,' they say, 'Unhealthy'. I imagine there were people who said this about Barbara.

So you see, fat or thin, you can't really win. About me they'd say, 'Unhappy, eating to compensate. Eating disorder.' About Barbara they'd say, 'Far too thin, probably starving herself to keep it that way. Eating disorder.' Because that's what people are like.

Did I focus on Barbara's thinness and envy her for it? The answer is no. My mother and father did all they could to encourage me to lose weight. They thought I would be happier and healthier and probably prettier (although they didn't say so) if I were thin. Actually, doing it was up to me, and I knew it.

~

My father may have had his moments when he thought he didn't look too bad, but one thing he certainly wasn't vain about at all was his feet. To be honest, his feet were nothing to write home about. They were really terrible to begin with and as if that wasn't enough, he had ingrown toenails and that just made things worse.

The first time I met Barbara properly (it was the second time we'd been in each other's presence but the first time was the time she was too shy to talk to me) was at her father's house in Inanda in Johannesburg. *'n Baie grand plek*: a very grand place indeed. We were all new to each other in those days. It was just prior to the wedding and my father and I were guests of Barbara's family, the Zoellners.

I badly wanted to be at the wedding. I don't think insisting on going was the most diplomatic thing I could have done at home, but all the same I insisted and being in a defiant frame of mind, I was glad I insisted. I don't think I fully realised until then that when my father left Zeekoevlei he didn't just move to another place: he moved into an entirely different world. It was amazing to me. I couldn't believe that this other, very grand, very glittering world had been there all the time, running parallel to our own, and I'd never known about it. I can tell you one thing. If you want a crash-course in what that world was like, you could have done worse than visit the Zoellner house where Barbara had grown up.

I had a dress my mother made. I was determined to wear it. Barbara didn't know about this. She said she would like to give me a dress as a gift and I could choose anything I wanted. If I'd ever been between the devil and the deep blue sea over this whole business before I really was now, but I said all right, I'd go and look at dresses with her, and we saw some really beautiful things.

I was quite warming to the idea. I'd never seen such a selection of dresses all in my size. It was rather comforting. There were so many big sizes to choose from and such lovely styles. Everyone knows that the bigger the size gets the more like a tent the dress becomes, but it seemed to my inexperienced eye that it was not so in the best shops of Johannesburg. You could get whatever you wanted and in sizes 44 upwards.

I didn't know what I was going to say to my mother if I took Barbara up on her offer, but as it happens, I didn't have to say anything at all. The shop Barbara took me to was so exclusive that the sizes on offer were all from Europe, where size 44 is actually what we would call a size 32. So I stuck with the outfit I'd brought and everyone was happy.

The Zoellners were very nice people and couldn't do enough to make us feel welcome. On our side, my father and I also wanted to play our part and make a good impression and show we knew how to behave properly and be good guests, so they wouldn't have the slightest reason to say anything bad about us behind our backs once we'd left.

Everything was wonderful the day we first had lunch at the Zoellners. They had invited a small party of people and we all sat outside and had drinks before lunch. There was gin and tonic and ice and lemon and everyone very polite to everyone else and I thought to myself that if I had never seen 'elegant' in my life before, I was surely seeing it now. Barbara was there, of course, looking tanned and beautiful with her lovely long hair hanging loose. She was absolutely glowing with happiness.

Lunch was beautifully prepared and everything set out just so. All we needed was a photographer to come and take a picture for a lifestyle magazine. It was just so perfect, they wouldn't even have needed to bring a stylist with them.

Everyone seemed thrilled with my father and he was enjoying himself and I was beginning to feel at ease, when someone suggested that we should all go down to the pool and have a swim to cool off before lunch.

That was the end of the world for my father because of The Feet. The Feet are maybe something a person would like to keep to himself until after the marriage vows are taken and all the documents signed. It was terrible. Everyone was so nice about everything that I could see there was no way my father was going to be able to put off the unveiling of this terrible problem of The Feet and I didn't know what he could do about it. I don't know what I thought might happen. I feared that maybe Barbara would run away screaming and change her mind about everything. Or even worse, I thought she might laugh. I felt so sorry for my poor father and just hoped everyone would realise that aside from The Feet he was not a bad-looking man. Really horrible feet are, after all, not the absolute end of the world.

In the end he came out in his swimming things with bandages around his toes and Barbara nearly had a heart attack. She thought he'd been in some terrible accident. He said he'd dropped a surfboard onto his feet. My mouth went open like a fish and I closed it again quickly. I don't think my father ever saw a surfboard in his life, but those were the early days. I suppose even though she was too polite and well brought up ever to broadcast it, Barbara found out about The Feet eventually and she married him just the same and everything was okay.

I was at the wedding just as I'd wanted to be, so I had my way, but my mother was still looking out for me. She wanted to make quite sure I didn't have my head completely turned. So she sent someone to fetch me, just in case somewhere along the way I'd forgotten where I belonged and wouldn't know how to find my way home again.

My mother at this time was worried about 'materialism'. I think she was very well aware that the parallel world I'd had such an enticing glimpse of existed and saw it as her responsibility to do what she could to save me from being sucked into it.

My mother thinks people ought to stay humble. I think it's probably not too bad an idea, but I really didn't think going to my father's wedding and being a part of a very important day in his life was putting my soul in any kind of jeopardy.

I wasn't in any trouble, anyway. I could never have afforded to live the kind of life the Zoellners lived. I wasn't trained for it either, and I'd already travelled too far down my own life's path by that time to make any drastic change of direction. My mother needn't even have given it a second thought. I was safe.

<hr>

Everyone knows Barbara was beautiful, but she was modest too and didn't like public display. When she and my father married she decided against a wedding cake that had already been ordered because it had been put on public display, in view of the celebrity status of the wedding.

It's hard to imagine that people are so interested in you that even your wedding cake is interesting enough to warrant attention from people you don't know from Adam and probably never will. Can you imagine someone you don't even know who would give two straws to know what your wedding cake looks like? This is what happened to Barbara, and she minded very much that the caterer had put her wedding cake on display. If everyone has seen something special before you've even seen it yourself, it takes something away from it, but Barbara wouldn't allow that to happen.

Because people were so interested in the cake she auctioned it for charity. She had another one made for her special day and because the first cake was used for a good cause, to raise money for people who could do with some help, I think that made it even more special for her.

It was her way.

She wasn't vain but she was a very elegant woman. For three years, in 1984, 1985 and 1988, she was on the *Sunday Times* Best Dressed list. On one of these occasions she won a prize of a trip overseas. She gave it as a treat to a young cancer-sufferer called Lerica de Villiers.

It was a gesture that was both natural to and typical of her. It is still very hard to believe that beautiful Barbara, who was a good wife, a wonderful mother and one of the most modest people you could ever hope to meet, was destined to be taken by a disease as cruel as cancer just over ten years later.

Life can be hard, but it is generous too sometimes and because you don't know what lies ahead you are spared knowing the end, so that nothing detracts from the good days.

In those days Barbara was at her most beautiful and she had a wonderful glow that seemed to float around her. My father was very proud of her and although the dynamics of my life had changed, in a very short time she fitted into the broad scheme of things so naturally that it seemed to me she'd always been there.

But in that short time there were some things I had to come to terms with. Our family, as I've told you, are not that great at communication. My brother and I in our separate ways had learnt of our parents' divorce and of my father's remarriage when we read the news on newspaper placards. As desirable ways of being told of a final and painful decision go, on a scale of one to ten, I would rate this pretty low down. My brother, who was doing his national service in the navy when news of my father's engagement to Barbara broke, was deeply distressed. The matter was so public that Admiral Biermann, then chief of the Navy, gave him a week's compassionate leave and sent him home to my mother for her to help him through it.

As you know, at the time of the divorce I was in Bloemfontein skiing in the SA Games and I suppose everyone read the same newspapers I did, knew all about it and was just too polite to mention it, so I just busked my way through. A coping strategy, I know, but it's one way of doing things when what you really feel is actually too private and painful to share.

It wasn't so easy when the announcement was made that my father was to marry Barbara. I was in residence at Stellenbosch University in a hostel called Huis Minerva. This is not the kind of news one wants to find out from a newspaper, but once again that was my lot in life and I heard of the change in our family arrangements by courtesy of the Fourth Estate.

I walked out of the residence one evening and saw a newspaper placard. You can't believe everything you read in newspapers, but I believed this.

You know about 'too much'? That really was too much. I don't mind not being at the centre of things. That's never been too much of a problem for me, but at that moment, being so peripheral seemed to me to make me count for very little indeed, and it hurt.

My life was changing around me and I had no power over any of it, no power at all. I began to walk and I began to cry. I cried a very great deal and just kept on walking.

I walked away from the residence where I stayed, down those famous streets lined with oaks. I suppose students before me had nursed broken hearts along just these same streets and for all kinds of different reasons. That's one thing. It's a very different thing when it happens to you.

The world goes on around you. The student haunts are full, there's lots of laughter and beer being drunk and fresh bottles of wine being opened, but that was happening to other people in some other life. It wasn't happening to me.

When holiday time came these students would all have families to go back to. Or so it seemed to me. I could imagine everyone except me going back to ordinary homes, the kind small children like to draw, with a mother and father and smiling children and smoke curling out of a chimney.

My home was not like that. It had not been like that for a long time, but despite the divorce it was still my home, my parents were still Dr and Mrs Barnard and that meant a lot to me. So it hurt. It hurt like anything. I couldn't believe the ordinariness of my pretty university town with its whitewashed buildings and Braak (village green) and the wonderful old church with its bell-chime. I had come here to blend in with other young people. Now I would be conspicuous again. The once-upon-a time waterskier whose father, that doctor who got rather too much attention, was now 'officially' getting divorced. I didn't want it but there was nothing I could do about it.

In later years a scene in the film *Forrest Gump* reminded me of myself at that time. It is the part where his mother tells him that he must keep on running until he gets the past behind him.

That was me too, but I didn't run, I walked. I walked until I couldn't walk any more. I walked until I came to the end of myself and I cried until I couldn't cry any more and I knew one thing. Not all the tears in the world would make any difference. The world – including my father's world and my own, which I knew would now be very different – would go on. I knew it and I knew it didn't make any difference which way I'd heard about this new change or any other changes that might come. There was nothing at all I could do about it.

Acceptance isn't something that comes in five minutes. It's a journey like any other and it's rocky and sometimes it's hard, but if you have the will for it you can get there.

In those days of my making peace with myself, with my life and with my father's life changes, I faced the one thing in life that was absolutely inevitable. What Forrest's mother said with such love and good faith in the film might have been true for him, but it isn't true for everyone.

You can't go on walking forever. At some point you have to go back, take what life has seen fit to send your way and make the best you can of it. My father was always going to be my father and, one way or another, a part of my life. I had choices. We all have choices, but in the matter of a father and daughter the *hardegat* attitude which would probably involve marginalising oneself and going into a kind of voluntary exile is really no choice at all. What would be the end result of that? I have seen children taking sides, estranging themselves from one parent or the other, and what happens to them? They stand on the outside feeling embittered and betrayed. That isn't me; besides which, I loved my father. Taking a deep breath and opening oneself up fully to all that life offers is the far better way, and learning in time not only to accept but actually to embrace those changes that happen to come your way is better still.

As it turned out, Barbara's coming into my life was far easier to accept than the above scenario might suggest because she was such a nice person. She was much more sophisticated than I was. I think it was the Continental thing again and the German way she had been brought up. She always behaved well. I have never seen one of her school report cards but I am sure her teachers would have said she was polite and dignified. She was all of that, and of course because of the way she looked, people looked at her. They just couldn't stop themselves and she was always very nice and she always looked wonderful, but this wasn't the only difference between us. There was one other thing and it was very important. On that famous cruise that we all took on board the *Chusan*, Barbara was the one who was married to that world-famous heart surgeon everyone was so anxious to have a piece of. Barbara was young when she married my father. It was a very busy life she came into and she had a full schedule of commitments and responsibilities. My life was very different and I was free as a bird.

I had a wonderful time on that cruise, but at the same time

something happened that was to make a big change in my life. I discovered and fell in love with Nutella. We didn't have Nutella in South Africa in those days and I had never come across it before. Have you ever eaten Nutella? What can I tell you? It was love at first bite, just as the advertisement for a totally different product tells you. No good at all for me with my weight problems, of course, but many young women go on cruise liners looking for love and romance. I didn't exactly find love and romance but I found Nutella, and it was almost as good. I suppose in its way it was the kind of love affair that could last a lifetime.

It was a very different time in my life when my father married his third wife, Karin, although there was some travel involved in that too.

My father invited Kobus and me to join him and Karin on a trip to Greece and Turkey. The invitation came a bit out of the blue, but that was part of the pleasure of it.

My father had made the acquaintance of the Setzkorns a very long time before, on one of our Buffels Bay holidays. Mrs Setzkorn asked my father, who was already a public figure at that time, if he would agree to have his photograph taken with her daughter. Of course he said he would, and there is a now-famous photograph of my father dandling the six-year-old Karin on his knee.

When she was seventeen Karin worked part-time as a waitress in the restaurant my father then had an interest in, but he was still married to Barbara at that time. It was only after the divorce, which had shaken him very badly, that they met again and the nature of their relationship began to change.

On Karin's 21st birthday my father gave her a party. We all knew by then that they were something rather more than friends, but it was an arrangement that seemed to suit them both. It was nice to see my father looking happy again with something of his old spark back.

My father's father, *Eerw.* Barnard

My father as a tennis champ

A family wedding in Paarl. Andre and me (on the right) and our cousins
(on the left)

Andre at Pretoria Boys' High

Me at Rustenburg Girls' High in my *tuisgebreide truitjie* (hand-knitted jersey). Thanks, Mom – *dankie, Ma!*

Adam, Ashlea, Ouma Louwtjie, Tiaan and Karen: my mother with the grandchildren contributed by Andre and Gail, Kobus and me

My Mother

Me and my Dad at Zeekoevlei

Back from Oz with a new friend. Second in the world and glad to be home

My days as a pin-up girl: how most people knew me then

Marilyn, me and Retha, just back from 'Jack Flax', in Minerva,
our residence at the University of Stellenbosch

The Mej. Viets competition: me with my 'chaperone', Annetjie Theron,
and all the princesses

Nanny days: Benjamin standing,
Joshua in the pram

Where would I have been without
Laura Ashley?

My cruising days: walking off the
gangplank of the *Chusan*

Andre as a first-year medical
student

I find Kobus ... ... and we are engaged

Family holidays at Buffels Bay

Andre and Ashlea

Me with my sister-in-law Gail and our children at Buffels Bay

A family holiday at Pringle Bay: Tiaan, Karen, Ashlea, Adam and Gail, with Frederick at the back with the hat on

My Dad and Barbara

With Madiba

With Princess Diana

The two 'little ones', Lara and Armin

The 'big boys', Frederick and Christiaan

What would the world be without friends you can rely on? (Left) Maureen Brink and my brother Andre; Father Tom in his 'come to Jesus' collar. (Below) Dene and me

TV interview in Stuttgart, 1997:
the thinnest I've ever been

Franscisca and me in the Ninon days

My Dad and me in Greece: in those days when I knew all the answers

'Skipskop': *die stukkies van my lewe lê deurmekaar*

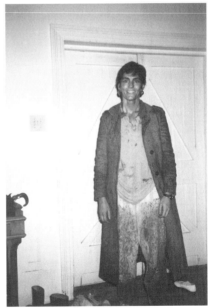

The Colour Purple: after the paint job by the SAP

Me and my family: Tiaan, Kobus, me and Karen on my Dad's 75th birthday at Beaufort West

Tiaan 'Dream on, Baby' Visser

Karen, the free-spirited daughter

As a surprise at the party he gave a slide show which recounted various stages of Karin's life until then. Of course the famous photograph of her sitting on his lap was one of the slides shown, and the music he'd chosen to accompany it was Maurice Chevalier singing 'Thank Heaven for Little Girls'. The grown-up Karin doing a 'reprise' of the original photograph, once again perched on his lap, followed this slide. The music my father chose to accompany this slide was the famous Beatles number 'When I'm Sixty-Four'.

It was hard to overlook the difference in their ages, and of course it was mentioned – politely to their faces and not so politely behind their backs.

The point is that they were happy with things as they stood and their decision was made. Most important of all was that out of that union came the two littlest Barnards, Armin Adam and Lara. These two, his youngest children, were Karin's great gift to him. They were the apple of his eye.

Just after he died, someone handed me a letter addressed to 'Dr Barnard's Daughter'. It was from the pianist at the hotel where he spent his last night. It was a very kind letter, intended for Lara, not for me. In it the pianist wrote that my father had asked her on that last night, more than once, to play 'Lara's Theme' for him and that she'd been happy to do so.

Lara is the youngest of my father's children and will never have the opportunity to spend as much time with him as I, who arrived on the scene first. That is a loss and I am sad for her because of it. I think one day that letter will be significant to her as a way of knowing that her father loved her and was thinking of her on that day just before he died.

Of course I knew none of this on that day in 1987 when Kobus and I boarded the plane with my father and Karin for our holiday in Turkey and Greece. My father had given no hint that there was anything special about this trip, but no sooner had the plane become airborne and the seatbelt lights been switched off than my father came to sit beside me.

He had something to ask me, he said. What he asked me was if I thought it would be all right if he married Karin. It was neither surprising nor unexpected, and yet in a way it was both. It was very different from standing in front of a newspaper placard in Stellenbosch, but I was different now too. What surprised me was that my father was a bit wary of me. At least that's what I felt. It was, I think, a bit of a role reversal. It made me feel adult, slightly surprised, slightly amused and as if something, a small ratchet somewhere in our relationship, had shifted just the tiniest bit.

Our visit to Greece was a happy one. Over the years my father had been generous in taking people along on trips with him. He'd taken Maureen and Fritz to Greece. My brother Andre and his wife Gail had been given a trip to Greece as well, and so had Karin's parents.

The usual gang of paparazzi followed my father. His marriage had him back on the front pages. We took a flight to the seaside town of Bodrum in Turkey and even there my father and Karin were front-page news.

Back in Greece, there were the newspapers. I couldn't read Greek but I could see the photographs of my father and Karin and the figures giving their respective ages, as well as a quote from Karin in which she said she didn't mind the age difference.

Kobus couldn't wait to slide away from the photographers and go off to explore. I stayed behind at the hotel and it was a very odd feeling. There seemed to be photographers just about wherever you looked and they all seemed to be getting tired and a little bit anxious. I don't know what their problem was. I suppose they had picture editors waiting for them to deliver, ready to tell them they weren't doing their jobs properly if they didn't come up with something.

It felt a bit like being a lion sitting in the Kruger Park minding your own business with all the tourists hanging around staring at you, just waiting for you to do something. I couldn't stand the suspense. I couldn't rush out and kill an impala or anything so I did what I considered the next best thing. I got up from where I was sitting, displaying myself in all my not insubstantial glory, and I jumped into the pool. That's me.

I looked like a baby whale. I looked like Christina Onassis when she was at her biggest. I thought that they – being paparazzi and Greek – must have spent a lot of time around Christina Onassis, and that maybe it would make them feel at home.

The truth is I felt sorry for them. You know that feeling at dinner parties when everyone is chewing and there's a terrible silence in the room and no one is quite certain what they're supposed to say next? That's how I felt. I felt I had to be the one to 'say' something.

It's ridiculous, but that's how it is, and that was the only photograph they got on that trip and to this day I am glad I don't read Greek because I would really hate to know how they decided to caption it.

After the divorce from Barbara my father had been a deeply unhappy man. Our friend Father Tom Nicholson, who has helped our family through many crises, said he was a 'broken reed', a man who needed healing, and it was Father Tom who counselled him at this time. 'It took hours, days and nights of sweat and tears and talking,' said Father Tom, 'but time, coupled with the acceptance of the thing we cannot change, proved once again to be a great healer.'

It may seem a strange thing to say in the light of what happened to my father in his life, but he was old-fashioned in many ways. He believed in the institution of marriage and he believed in the family.

So he was shattered when he and my mother eventually made their break after he'd been to the famous Red Cross Ball in Monaco.

He was a special guest of Prince Rainier and Princess Grace. The ball was a glittering affair. There was a cabaret by Charles Aznavour and, by his own admission, what he enjoyed most was dancing with Princess Grace.

I don't know what my father's dreams had been when he was a child but I think we can be pretty sure that when he was sitting in the bioscope in Beaufort West looking at Grace Kelly up on the silver screen, he never imagined that one day he'd be dancing with her.

The glamorous new life was now in full swing and everyone wanted to meet him. Those two sides of him that were to plague him all his life – the natural, barefoot boy from Beaufort West and the superstar surgeon – had started their long war with each other. In my opinion, he was destined to be at war with himself in this way for the rest of his life.

He felt 'guilty', he wrote afterwards. He felt guilty because while he was having a wonderful time my mother was 'sitting miserably' at home.

I am not sure that miserably is quite the right word. 'Furiously' might have been better. When my father came back from that trip and his friend Stoffie Stoffberg picked him up at the airport, Stoffie had news for him.

'All your belongings are in the boot of the car,' he said. 'Louwtjie has thrown them – and you – out of the house and she says she doesn't want you back. I packed as much as I could in the time I had.'

My father was in San Francisco promoting a book called *The Body Machine*, which he'd co-authored, when Noel Tunbridge, his lawyer, phoned him to tell him he had some bad news for him.

Barbara's lawyer had just telephoned him. She was suing for divorce. Once again, my father was back where he started.

'I was thrown out of my home – just as it had been with Louwtjie. This time I had only my clothes and three pieces of furniture: a chair I had inherited from my parents, a chair that Barbara's mother gave us and a writing desk her father had given me.'

When the end came with Karin it was not all that much different. All his belongings were packed up in cardboard boxes and set out ready for him to remove them. In that instance it was my sister-in-law Gail who went to collect them.

My poor father! With him it seemed that as far as married life was concerned, it was always back to square one again.

When the marriage to Barbara ended it was Maureen Brink who came to the rescue. She had a guest house called Rockhaven out at Blaauwberg beach, where the view of Table Mountain is so marvellous. He went to stay there.

He said he would have done anything to win Barbara back, but Barbara had made her decision and it wasn't to be. I think Barbara married my father because she loved him and because she was slightly dazzled by him. Travel was nothing new to her and through her parents she already knew a great many interesting people. But I'm quite sure my father added a new dimension to this, and while she was comfortable with it – you might even say almost born for it – Barbara was never someone who deliberately looked for celebrity.

She had said more than once that she would have been perfectly happy living a quiet life on the farm they owned down at Sedgefield on the southern Cape coast, where she'd be free to enjoy family life. I have no doubt she meant it, but it didn't happen that way.

My father, if you can believe it, wrote that he'd envisaged Barbara sitting alone at home after the divorce fretting over the loss of her 'wonderful husband', which just goes to show that his ideas about women were pretty outdated.

Perhaps it was a generational thing. I can't, for example, imagine one of my daughter's boyfriends entertaining such thoughts about her!

All the same, it was something that was very hard for him to face up to. He couldn't bear the idea that there would ever be anyone else in Barbara's life, but of course she was a beautiful woman and a very nice person and it was inevitable that in time she would meet someone else. So it was not really surprising when she met and married Joe Silva.

I don't know how long it took before my father realised that the life he and Barbara had together was truly over. I think it may have been the evening he went back to Waiohai, the house in Constantia they'd once shared and Joe – who was a frequent visitor there – offered him a drink.

My father was the trespasser in what had once been his home, and Joe was the host. When Barbara, who had left the room to get ready for dinner, came back and asked him please to excuse them as they were about to eat, I think he finally realised that it truly was over.

When my father told me that he intended formalising his relationship with Karin I was glad he would be given the chance of being happy again. This is what I told him. I was grateful to Karin for loving him and accepting his proposal of marriage. I told him this too. I meant every word of it then and I mean it still.

At this stage he was just about to retire from Groote Schuur Hospital. Ahead of him lay a two-year stint at the Baptist Medical Centre in Oklahoma City, where he was to establish a heart unit. He bought his farms in the Karoo and brought the full force of his energy to that project, stocking them with every kind of wildlife, even rhinoceros. In between all this there was to be a great deal more international travel, as well as lectures, speeches and books to write.

He needed a companion and a helpmeet and Karin gave him joy and his much-loved last little family. Sitting on the plane that day I said to him what I had said to him so many times before, which was that he should do what he thought would make him happy. His happiness was then, as it had always been, my only concern.

⁓

I sometimes think about what 'beautiful' really means. My friend Francisca (Frankie) is beautiful in a Spanish way. That was what I thought the first time I met her. She was beautiful not just because of her looks, which are very fine, but because she had such style, and real style is not something you phone up and order from Verimark. She's got 'it' and so has my friend Bella, which is just about the best name she could possibly have. She's beautiful and she's something else too: when she invites you into her space, wherever that space happens to be, you feel special and you feel safe.

Caro Wiese is another friend of mine who is beautiful. She is beautiful not just because she happens to have been ladled out a fair share of good looks when she was born. It is more than that. Caro is beautiful because she has a kind heart and a generous spirit. She is a friend in need and no one knows how to make moments of magic the way Caro does, except maybe my Dad and David Copperfield.

I don't know why people are so bothered by fat, but they are. The poor little fat one is always a little bit out. Even children pick up on this and if there isn't some adult around who's mindful of it, children can turn on their chubbier peers, make their lives extremely miserable and maybe even damage their self-concept for life.

I know what I'm talking about. At the beginning of my school career we did our gym in school bloomers and I knew even then I was different. I had a friend called Linda Eglin whose legs didn't touch at the top, and mine did. We weren't the same shape at all, which I knew was not the best news as far as I was concerned.

It was exactly the same thing I was to rediscover later in my life after I won the Mej. Viets competition and posed for the cover of *Foto-Rapport*. You can slide one knee over another just as much as you like, but there are few things in life more difficult to conceal than a nice plump juicy thigh that simply refuses to be hidden.

When I was a child we were encouraged to think of children less fortunate than we were and to eat everything on our plates. While we were doing it I suppose we had to hope that some guardian angel somewhere had had the forethought to provide us with mothers who knew what balanced nutrition was.

Nowadays people have praise lavished on them for losing weight – the thinner the better. It's hard to say which is more dangerous.

Yet I remember meeting what most people would call a fat girl once. I was at a very yuppie kind of lunch party in Cape Town and in the middle of the lunch this girl arrived. She'd just come in from a walk on the mountain. She was wearing Caterpillar shoes and shorts and she seemed to bloom with self-confidence and health and happiness. You couldn't help liking her. Everyone responded to her, and even though they were surrounded by thin, pretty women all decked out like Christmas trees for the occasion, the men were really enjoying her. She made me feel so good. I wanted to stand up and just say out loud that it was time to 'come back, Rubens, all is forgiven'. If Beryl Cook had been there she would have been reaching for her sketch book.

Seeing that girl taught me a lesson. Big women are beautiful too. I've seen it with my own eyes more than once and I really should remember it. I feel so sad when I see a big woman trying to hide in a big tent of a dress that looks as if she shopped for it at

Tent & Tarpaulin. I've been there myself in my Laura Ashley days and I know what it feels like.

A straight A plus to the well proportioned Venus of Camps Bay Beach, my friend Lizzie Simon. She comes down to the sand in a white towelling robe with a straw hat on her head, designer sunglasses on her face, carrying a beautiful basket with her things in it, and with really nice earrings clipped to her ears. She's the last word in style and it's lovely to see it.

9

What's in a name?

Queen Victoria didn't like the idea of telephones.
'Does it mean people may actually speak to you in
your own home?' If Queen Victoria were with us
today, would I have a few things to tell her!

If anyone were to ask me if I loved my father I would say yes; yes,
I did. Many people did and there were just as many who could
hardly bear to hear his name mentioned. People said he was ego-
tistical, vain and self-centred.

When someone was asked to contribute to *Chris Barnard: By*
Those Who Know Him by David Cooper, they said: 'I have decided
against contributing for a number of reasons. Suffice it to say that
if Chris was a more sympathetic human being and not only interested in Chris Barnard I would gladly have participated.'

A great many things were said about him. Some were probably
true, a great many were totally untrue and some of them were
deeply personal and very hurtful to our family and to me.

I feel great sympathy for families who have one of their members in the spotlight. I think about Princess Diana and her sons.
My father had met Princess Diana and liked her very much. Even
now, several years after her death, books are still being written
about her – some of which I have read – that have made her two

sons incandescent with anger. I feel nothing but sympathy for them and can imagine just how furious they are and how helpless they feel.

It's already been written about in one of the books published after her death that she and my father had a correspondence. This is true, and when my father died I inherited his personal papers and the letters along with them.

I've never read them.

It says in the book that the Princess wanted my father to help her help a friend. It's simple enough. In fact, it's the kind of thing people do every day, and if they hadn't happened to be two people who found themselves on someone's Internet list of the two hundred great icons of the twentieth century, there's no one who'd even think twice about it. They'd call it networking, push the delete button and get on with their lives, but that is in the normal, everyday world. It has no place in the world the Princess and my father inhabited.

I wasn't surprised then to receive several telephone calls from journalists who knew of the existence of the correspondence and badly wanted to know what was in it.

One journalist telephoned from London and, having established that my father had indeed known the late Princess and had corresponded with her, asked if I realised how exciting this was. She said that if she were in possession of such documents she'd 'pee in her pants'.

I don't think this is a urological problem. In fact, I think it's some kind of journalistic epidemic. Clearly this is the effect an icon like Princess Diana has upon certain female journalists.

Another journalist, a man, to whom my family were extremely generous with time and help, also had his eye on the letters. They were the hook he might use, he explained, to sell the concept of a biography of my father to a big London publisher. When it became clear that we were happy to be truthful about their existence but unwilling either to hand them over or have them made public, he felt we had let him down in some way. He had a wife and family to support, a state of affairs with which we were fully in sympathy.

At the end of the day journalists are themselves subject to the same kinds of bias and self-interest that they so often seek to expose in their subjects.

Funnily enough, my father has a photograph of himself standing next to President Mandela. It was taken late in his life and people sometimes remark that they appear to be more or less the same height. Perhaps they are, but I live with that photograph and it always looks to me as if they're two men who've reached a certain time in their lives; and it looks as if they're propping each other up.

President Mandela is a very famous person. I don't think anyone can argue with the fact that he's an icon, but I've never had any phone calls asking for a 'story behind the story' on that particular picture. I wonder why? After all, President Mandela is the famous person's famous person. Perhaps it's because Mandela seems to have conducted his life for so long with absolute probity, so that he sets a shining example to the world. It's those public icons who turn out to be as fallible as the rest of us who are pursued relentlessly by the media.

We have always been helpful towards journalists. I don't think that in my own case it's done me much good. All it has really done for me is give me a reputation for being the kind of person who can't say no. That's true, but not necessarily a good thing. In the end, all that being over-anxious to please does is backfire on you.

It has become clear to me over a period of time that you can end up being denounced by the press as only one of two things. Either you are grubbing for publicity and can't wait for the next centimetre of newsprint to appear, or you are 'not cooperative', and who do you think you are anyway? Which seems to me, whichever way you look at it, to be a no-win situation. These journalists argue that in exposing the vulnerabilities of others – in as civilised a way as they can, of course – they are only earning a living, after all. I hope that journalist found some other way to feed his family. I'm sure he did. He struck me as being both focused and resourceful.

On the matter of those letters, perhaps this is the best place to state exactly why we choose to keep them private and since my father's papers came to me, perhaps I'm the one who can best explain this.

We are, in our family, the children of a man not unfamiliar with media attention. Sir Roy Calne, one of the world's best-known liver and kidney transplant surgeons, and also the author who so efficiently dealt with my father in Chapter 3, called him the Film Star Surgeon.

> Being naturally good looking and enjoying the limelight of the media, his public appearances tended to be similar to those of a film star rather than a surgeon. All his dealings with non-medical people were highly successful, well publicised and brought him much criticism from colleagues who felt that public adulation of a surgeon is not appropriate.

'Oh yes, but he loved it!' people say with a sneer, and perhaps it was so. There are people who say the same thing about Princess Diana. But the point is no one really takes into consideration how the children might feel. And this is why we shall never allow these letters to be published.

Not all the things said about my father were sarcastic or negative, a great many positive and admiring things were said and written about him too. There's absolutely no doubt about it: he had his fans.

My father knew a great many people. Far too many, some people might say. He certainly knew far more people from right across the spectrum of life than the average person does.

I am forever picking people up. It drives my son crazy. He can't stand what he calls 'hullo, hullo'. When we're out together and people start moving in our direction to come and say 'hi' to us, he's already pulling at my arm, saying we should move in the other direction.

'I'm not in the mood for "hullo, hullo" today,' is what he always says. I understand how he feels. I have tried to improve. When I'm walking around on my own, though, I have no deterrent. I love talking to people. I like talking to street people, they always have such heart-rending stories to tell and inevitably I feel sorry for them and end up asking them home with me, so I can give them something to eat and maybe a few old clothes.

In those months just before my father died I met a *bergie* outside in the road. If you don't know Cape Town you may not know what *bergies* are. Technically, they are vagrants and scavengers. They drink too much cheap wine if they ever get the chance to lay their hands on it. They scratch around in refuse bins to see what they can get to eat or what they can find to sell. They sleep rough and take life as it comes.

We call them *bergies* here in Cape Town because many of them live on our mountain. We say it with affection. *Bergies* don't harm anyone and they don't steal. If you can say anything about them you could say they were even a little bit shy of people. If you give them something they will receive it with cupped hands and thank you profusely with their voices, with their eyes and more often than not with a bare-gummed smile.

The *bergie* whom I met just before my father died told me his name was Michael. He said he was a gardener by trade and that he came from the Eastern Cape and couldn't find work. I struck up a conversation with him and said I would find him a garden job to help him get a small amount of money, and he was grateful for this, so I took him to my father's house. I thought we could arrange some work in the garden there, and my father was happy to see him.

It was very early in the morning. My father was in his dressing gown in the kitchen. He wasn't looking his best. He'd had the disfiguring cancer that required his nose to be rebuilt. He was busy about the kitchen doing the best he could with his arthritic hands that were there on display for anyone to see. The terrible feet were on display too. Michael's whole face lit up as he recognised him.

'Aren't you Dr Barnard?' he said. When my father said he was, Michael immediately demanded that I find a camera somewhere, and asked if my father would be good enough to pose with him for a picture and if I would see that he got a copy of it to show his friends. My father was happy to oblige and I did as he requested.

My father knew a great many people. It wasn't the celebrities he was interested in, it was the kind of people they actually were that concerned him. I wonder as I write this how many of those people he knew actually knew him in return.

I was asked if I'd like to put my views of him into a book where everyone writes about the Barnard they knew. I declined, although plenty of others were happy enough to dash off a little bit of Barnard. I don't think my father would have minded and I certainly had some things I could have said, but I said no because I thought it was an assault on my father's private space.

Everyone seems to choose the 'Chris Barnard' that happens to suit them best, and because he had many facets to his personality it's easy enough to mix and match as much as you want until you get the best fit.

I'm quite sure I do the same and that what I write about now is the 'Chris Barnard' I choose. I think I know now why all those other people were out there picking and choosing to construct the

'Prof. Barnard' they wanted. It's because out of his many gifts, the one true gift he had was his ability to make magic. My father, when he wished, had the power to make my life magical, and he did.

10

The Colour Purple

*The Colour Purple is a famous book by
Alice Walker. It's also what happened in the old
South Africa if you decided the time had come
for you to stand up and protest*

Between teaching at the Monterey Pre-Primary School and doing
the correspondence course that qualified me as a remedial teacher
and enabled me to work first at St Agnes and later at Herzlia, I did
a small stint in the fashion business.

Personally, I am not going to put Claudia Schiffer out of business, but I have in my life been around people who could certainly
have given her a run for her money.

Maybe it started off with the Sunday School clothes. My
mother, I've told you, is a wonderful needlewoman. Nothing
leaves Louwtjie Barnard's hands – not her children all dressed up
in their Sunday best or a life-saving heart valve to be sewn into
someone she doesn't even know – unless it is perfect.

So I learnt first from my mother. And then I learnt from
Barbara. There's no doubt at all about that. Without Barbara I
might have come this far in my life and not have known what a
Pucci print was.

Barbara was my age – there were only three months between us

– but she was not like me. Or, maybe I should say I was not like her. Barbara exuded style. She didn't even have to work at it and she had exquisite taste.

Whenever I spent even five minutes in her company I made up my mind that what I wanted more than anything in the world was to be just like her.

I'd go to the shops and look for things that looked 'Barbara-ish', and that was back to reality with a shock because to acquire the kind of style that came to her quite naturally didn't come cheap. Even if I could have got it together, it was way out of my price bracket.

None of which says I wasn't free to learn from her. I didn't want to copy her. No one could have done that. When I was with Barbara, what I wanted to do was stand still and see if I could absorb some of her world through osmosis. This is what exposure to another world does to one and I consider myself lucky to have had that opportunity.

As I've already said, I have always admired what I regard as a Continental look. In my waterskiing days, when I did a lot of travelling, it was something you couldn't fail to notice when you walked down the streets of Europe. Everyone – particularly the women – was so well dressed. I didn't know what it was they were doing that made them look that way. All I knew was that it was something I hadn't been aware of in South Africa, and I admired it very much.

I wasn't the only one who admired Barbara's taste, by the way. Just about everyone who saw her did, those who knew what they were talking about and those who didn't. Those who did persuaded her to open a shop – not just any old shop, Barbara would never have done that – but a designer boutique that catered for people like herself (or people who aspired to be like her) and reflected her own taste.

In the early days of her married life Barbara opened B&B

Boutique in the Golden Acre, Cape Town. She started it with a friend of hers called Bertha, which is where the other B came from. It was very chic in those days and people came to look and, if they could afford it, to buy. People came to look at Barbara as much as anything else because she was very hands-on in the shop, because that was her nature. When she did something she took pride in it and liked it to be perfect.

Sometimes people who were a bit intimidated by the look of the shop – and I suppose to a certain extent by Barbara herself – would just peer in through the window, pretending they were looking at the clothes just so they could see her. It was not the kind of thing she liked, but if she minded she didn't let on. Barbara never sought out the limelight. Once she found herself in it she was just herself, as if she had been born to it, but no matter what her life might have been or what other kind of life she might have had if she hadn't married my father, people would have looked at her anyway. That's just the way it was.

When I was pregnant with Karen she offered me a job doing part-time work in her boutique. I must say that in my life, Barbara was very often the one to come to the rescue. When I didn't have a job I looked after Frederick and Christiaan and she insisted on paying me for it. Everyone seemed to have an opinion about it. I really don't know why.

'How can you take money for looking after your own half-brothers?' they'd say, scandalised. 'How could "she" offer it to you?'

The shrinks will tell you that you do this kind of thing because you seek acceptance and maybe there is some element of truth in that. After all, they don't go to university and study to be psychiatrists without learning something about what motivates people. Perhaps there is an element of wanting to be liked and wanting to be accepted. I accept that (see what an accepting person I am!).

I will tell you that in the first place Barbara was Barbara. She was never 'she' to me and she was sensitive to my situation and she always urged me to buy something nice for myself with the money she paid me. I liked being a big sister cum nanny to her boys and no matter what her own feelings might have been, she indulged me and allowed me to be that. I think that says a great deal about her.

Finally, despite what the shrinks say, you do things because you want to do them. After all, you can always say no.

As far as the money is concerned, this was Barbara's way of tactfully seeing I had extra pocket money and not simply offering a handout, and I liked being with my half-brothers and so it was not only useful but also extremely pleasant for me.

When I was governessing some time later for an artist with her dyslexic son, it was Barbara who told me about the post coming open at the Monterey school and so paved the way for my first teaching job. When she asked me if I'd like to help out at B & B during my pregnancy, she was coming to my rescue again. She could have asked anyone, but she didn't, she asked me. I got to be in a smart shop, among nice things, plain and pregnant and absolutely enormous in Helanca (do you remember Helanca material?) surrounded by garments by Ungaro and other beautiful things definitely not destined for the washline in the backyard, because they were made entirely of silk.

If I say so myself, I was an excellent saleswoman. I could sell ice in winter and I still can, except these days I do it for fund-raising purposes. I like to think that seeing me around the shop gave people the confidence to come in and look around. I am lots of things in this life, but I don't think intimidating is one of them.

It wasn't above me to step out into the mall and drag people inside and insist they have a better look. I understand very well how nice it is to be among beautiful things even if you can't afford them. Just because you don't have the money to buy something doesn't mean you don't appreciate it. Most of the world can't afford to buy a Van Gogh but that doesn't mean they don't flock in their millions to art galleries all over the world just to have a look. I liked my time in B&B. It opened a new door for me.

Of course, I still had to go and push my babies out and I pushed very hard, let me tell you. I think because I didn't pay proper attention to what my breathing teacher told me. Do things my own way, that's me, and with my babies as with so many other things in my life, doing things my way didn't pay the best dividends.

I came out of my confinements with my veins standing out like a route map all over my face and my neck. My father and Barbara came to the Mowbray Maternity Hospital to see me and were horrified. My father actually wrote in one of his books that it was my own fault and that I should have paid more attention in my prenatal classes, and he was right.

Barbara, by the way, also gave birth to her boys at the Mowbray Maternity Hospital, which was a state hospital. She could have gone anywhere she chose but she chose to go there and that too was exactly like her. She had married a man who'd elected to stay in the employ of the state so that his services were always freely available to anyone who needed them. Barbara respected this and her respect didn't just take the form of lip service. If a state hospital was good enough for my father's patients, she considered it was more than good enough for her to bring his children into the world.

~

After I became a mother and was looking for something gainful to do, fashion became part of my life once again.

Sometimes women in Cape Town get together at each other's houses to look at little one-off items. Sometimes it's something someone has brought in from Europe and sells to make a little extra pin money. Sometimes it's because someone can make something really special and beautiful and everyone is looking for something you don't see every day when you walk through the shopping malls.

It was at one of these functions that I got started again. By this time I'd been around Barbara and her Pucci things and the Ungaro in B&B. I'd met Elzbieta Rosenwerth, who made my mother's dress for my wedding, and you must know that if anyone can make something good enough for my mother they just have to be the best. I suppose this wouldn't look like too much of a CV if you were recruiting for Armani, but I felt quite comfortable about it.

There I was at this get-together and this woman called Frankie walked in, and she had The Look – that European look I so admired. I have said elsewhere in this book that Francisca is a very beautiful woman with an amazing sense of style, as well as the kind of presence that is a fashion statement all by itself. Frankie and I were to become friends, as well as partners in our boutique, Ninon, which was named after her daughter.

~

Frankie would put things together for people, creating a look, taking a sow's ear and making a silk purse out of it. On the other hand, I have always been natural. And when you have a son like mine you know exactly how far natural is likely to get you.

When he was younger he was lying in the bath when I came into the bathroom to put cream on my legs.

'What are you doing?' he asked.

You can see he wasn't a boy accustomed to seeing his mother in any of the many processes that go with beautification. (I hope it doesn't ruin women for him forever, but I'm sure it won't.)

'What I'm doing is creaming my rather beautiful legs,' I told him. He looked at me and gave it at least a minute's thought before he said: 'Dream on, baby, dream on.'

Clearly neither my legs – nor my attitude – gained any kind of seal of approval from my son. Mind you, in the interest of family relations, he might for the sake of peace have lied. Not a big lie –

just a small one would have done – but I'm glad he didn't and would have been surprised if he had. About matters like this, we in our family have always been forthright.

Sometimes it's a bit too much for most people to take, but that's the way we are. 'Frank' is a good word for it, I would say. Very frank is probably better. I'll give you an example.

Every year, on the anniversary of my brother's death, my mother, my daughter Karen, my son Tiaan and I go to the Garden of Remembrance to place flowers at the place where his ashes are kept.

Each year I ask my children if either of them would like to say a prayer for their uncle. The first time we did this Karen said a lovely little prayer. Then Tiaan, praying out loud, said: 'Dear God, thank you so much that you took Ouma's son and not her daughter, otherwise I would not have had a mamma.'

Which, I suppose, is one way of putting it. My brother would have found it quite funny, I think. As for me, despite the fact that my efforts at beautification didn't impress him all that much, it's still good to know your son values you. Even if the compliment is an extremely back-handed one!

My daughter is a bit like me, at least in so far as beautification goes. We are not really dress-up people and no one would ever think I'd just stepped off the cover of *Vogue*. But every now and then even I have to get myself together and go out looking vaguely respectable, so I thought I could do with someone like Frankie in my life to 'put me together', and I started buying from her.

Her work was wonderful and her prices were reasonable but I soon realised that she was making things for next to nothing and selling them so that they were ending up in shops at many times what she'd charged for them. It didn't make sense, so I suggested to her that she start up a business, make only for herself and sell her things through her own outlet.

It was not my original intention to go into business with her.

'I'll help you,' I said, and I did, and it went so well that I gave up teaching and went into the business with her. I loved the business and the selling side of it, so that's what I did and Frankie and a small team of seamstresses just kept turning out the kinds of clothes the women of Cape Town liked to wear. Sometimes they brought along their out-of-town friends too. It was a happy shop. In fact, I shouldn't really call it a shop at all because it really was something quite different.

Our clients (we were rather exclusive and called our customers clients) used to pop in for a chat. They'd pop in for a cup of coffee. They'd tell us what was going on in their lives. We talked about clothes and husbands and the problems with children and in-laws and home help and money. You name it, at Ninon we talked about it, so you can see we really trafficked in a lot more than just clothes, but we sold clothes as well.

Barbara bought from us sometimes. When things changed in my father's life and Karin was part of it she bought from us and she modelled for us too. We gave regular fashion shows so that our clients could get together and talk on a larger scale and also see what was going to be in the shop the next season.

My mother worked in the shop on Saturday mornings to give us a break and she didn't mind providing the tea or the coffee and the good advice, and all in all it was a bit 'Barnardy' although Frankie with her wonderful style was always the creative force.

The late Marike de Klerk, who was very much in the full flower of her prominence then, came in for a shop. She bought an outfit from us that we thought was quite wonderful. We imagined her appearing in it at all kinds of smart functions – until she told us that she thought it was perfect for just chilling out in at her holiday home. That's what she'd come in to look for and that, in her opinion, was what she went out with. Which was Frankie and me put well and truly and firmly in our place!

Ninon, sitting on its little suburban corner under the mountain, was a happy place. I think anyone who knew it in its heyday would agree that whether they walked out with a carrier bag and a nice new outfit or not, when they left they felt better than when they arrived.

Ultimately, Ninon came to an end because all things run their course and one needs to move on. With a shop like Ninon you have a good time, you become flavour of the month, and then you have to keep reinventing yourself because obviously you want to keep your customers happy and keep up a standard. Then one day you wake up and think you'd actually quite like to move on, and it's good to do it while you're still ahead of the game.

So that's what we did. Francisca had things she wanted to do and frankly, much as I'd enjoyed myself, my heart really lay with teaching and working with children. I wanted to get back to it. Neither of us ever wanted Ninon to become a 'business-business' or a chore. We wanted it to be a successful business, of course, and it was that, but more than that, we wanted it to be fun. I have already indicated that it has a kind of *kaffeeklatsch* feel about it, and it did, but it ran very much on our energies and the day came when we wanted to use our energies elsewhere. Our clients were rather sad when it ended, but we never felt we were closing a door that we could never open again. If we wanted to we could start up again. Nothing prevents us, and we have discussed it, but so far we are both happy with the direction our lives have taken and so, although anything is possible, perhaps our lives in fashion have run their course. But, as you know by now, I never say 'never'.

There was an election during the time Frankie and I worked together and we decided to offer our support and our window space to the Democratic Party, one of the parties that opposed the then National Party Government. I had in the past been a member of its predecessor, the Progressive Federal Party, which had also been in opposition to the Nationalists, but by the time that election came around the DP seemed better to reflect the kind of change many of us were so desperately looking for.

To show our support we decorated the shop window in blue and yellow, which were the DP colours.

There was a bit of political manoeuvring going on at the time, which in the light of all that came after seems pretty inconsequential, although at the time it seemed like a big thing.

A DP Member of Parliament called Tiaan van der Merwe was asked by the Nationalists to hold a watching brief for them and give them a reportback on an ANC rally. I suppose they wanted to know what was happening but, not wanting to be seen in the enemy camp, didn't want to send any of their own people along. Tiaan was under the impression that they were sending him only because they thought he could be relied on to be an honest broker.

In any event, it didn't turn out that way. The whole thing backfired and Tiaan was singled out at the rally as being an ANC supporter. I suppose the Nationalists thought they could make some political capital out of it and maybe turn some of his supporters against him.

As I say, it was a long time ago and in the light of the great changes that have taken place in this country, it was no great shakes by itself. But this is where I come into this story: the DP issued a press release on the matter and asked me if I could take it into the centre of town where the newspaper offices are.

I was happy enough to do it.

Off I went in my tracksuit, planning to walk down to town, do what I had to and then come back again, but when I got to town it became very clear that something big was on the go.

There were literally thousands of people gathered on the old cobbles of Greenmarket Square. These days it plays host to a street market and there's a nice buzz, with lots of people coming and going. Every day at midday, when the Noon Gun on Signal Hill is fired, the pigeons on the square flutter up and hang in the air for a while. Then they settle down again and go about the business of city birds, picking around between feet for whatever they can get.

It wasn't like that on that day.

All the thousands of people who'd gathered there in protest were carrying placards and singing, linking arms with each other and shouting out slogans. I don't know what happened to me, really. It was just the most marvellous feeling. I felt, just for a change, as if someone was actually giving voice to the pent-up frustration we all felt. It was like that in those days. There were a great many people of all colours, from all walks of life and from all strata of society, who were beginning to think that although we believed we stood right on the brink of change, it would never actually happen. Or if it happened it would arrive too late and people fed up with waiting would take to the streets and not just to sing and protest.

In any case, I thought just so far and no further. It was the same kind of thing that had happened to me in my university days. I had never been highly 'politicised' but I'd always been 'there'. Maybe a shrink would say that was because I wanted approval, but it wasn't like that. It was another feeling altogether. I simply could not comprehend 'apartness'. It was totally outside my frame of reference. I knew it to be wrong in every way and totally indefensible. I knew there was a great force that felt very differently. As for me, I felt very small. I tried to live always as my parents had taught me, in mutual respect with everyone. The things that I did were small things and changed, I know with great certainty, nothing at all.

One thing occurs to me, though. If everyone had done exactly the same, things might have gone better with us and we might have been able, after it was all gone and dismantled, to live more easily with ourselves in that different kind of country that came after.

That was the future, though. On that day I am telling you about, something in me told me that I was seeing history in the making in a far more forceful and accessible way than any number of press releases would ever reflect. I forgot all about my mission to Newspaper House. I joined in with the protesters with my undelivered press release still in my hand.

For a while it was good. One felt a sense of solidarity, of being involved in something good that was bigger than oneself. I know it may sound funny now, but I felt that just by being there I was standing up to be counted and actually doing something. It was a small thing but at least it was public and surely every small action – aligning oneself with an opposition party, carrying a press release, joining a protest rally – counts for something. A small something perhaps, but at least that's better than nothing at all. Of course, it couldn't last and it didn't.

Greenmarket Square has several streets that feed into it and down one of these streets came a kind of rumbling sound that I knew couldn't mean good news. A huge water cannon appeared, rolling right onto the Square. It came to a halt, directed its nozzle and let loose a huge jet of purple spray. There was no way of ducking it. The spray itself was harmless enough: it wasn't toxic or anything. But people started yelling and trying to get out of the way, but there was nowhere to go, there were just too many of us and there was nowhere we could go anyway.

Behind the cannon came the riot policemen and I don't know if you've ever seen a South African riot policeman up close or know what they looked like in their heyday, but if you've got any sense at all you don't mess with them. You wouldn't need to hear it from me. One look at them and you'd work it out quickly enough all by yourself.

In any case, I got furious. I stood there thinking, to hell with it. What a damn cheek they've got to do this. Nobody had done anything wrong. People were just sitting there, singing little songs, making their voices heard, exercising the right to protest which should be every citizen's.

There was a kind of movement and out of nowhere, it seemed, people joined hands and made a chain, holding tight onto each other and marching towards the cannon. Someone offered me a hand and I took it.

Then things became chaotic. The riot police fired teargas into the crowd and it burns like you can't imagine and half-blinds you and makes you choke. People started running and someone grabbed hold of me. I couldn't see who the person was. I couldn't see anything much at all because my eyes were streaming from the teargas but I could hear a voice in between all the shouting from both sides and the voice just kept saying over and over, 'You must be careful.'

That day, although I didn't know it then, the authorities had been expecting some kind of demonstration, and to augment their own forces they had brought in additional riot police from Pretoria.

The human chain had broken apart as chains will once the teargas hits them and the riot police advance, and the man with the disembodied voice holding my hand said: 'Come with me.' We made a dash for it, or at least as much of a dash as we could, considering the absolute chaos all around us.

Greenmarket Square is at the heart of the old town. Most of the buildings around there have old-fashioned doors and small lobbies with stairs and not lifts to take you to the upper floors.

We managed to find a building and get inside it. We sat on some steps that ran up from the lobby and tried to pull ourselves together, and at least we were out of it, but not for long.

The door, which we'd closed behind us, was booted open with a terrible *kadoef* sound and standing in the doorway was one of those Pretoria riot policemen I was talking about.

'Vandag, julle donners, moer ek vir julle.'

Which means (translated for family consumption), 'Today's the day you get your come-uppance.'

I don't know what usually happens to a person in a situation like this, but I know what happened to me. If I was furious before I was more than furious now. Here was this man, speaking to me in the language of my father and mother, in the language of my missionary grandfather, in the tongue of my mother's mother, who had such respect for words and used to read poetry.

You know, it's quite funny really, it's the Calvinist thing, I suppose, but even in a situation like that you remember what your mother told you about being polite. I am not a prissy woman but when in doubt, I always revert to polite.

'Ekskuus meneer,' I said. *'Maar hoe durf jy so vloek?'*

Which means, 'Excuse me, sir, but how dare you swear like that?' After all, you have to say something.

*'Kom hier, jou f***** voorbok.'* (Which translated has something to do with being a ringleader, expletive deleted.) With which he zapped me down and hit me with a baton. Then he pulled me out into the street and down the road to where a police van was standing. He pushed me into the back of the van and left me in there.

It was interesting, really. From where I sat I had a good and safe view and I saw a few things that will stay with me all my life.

The first thing I realised was that I had been lucky. They got me out of the way and put me where I was because I was white. The blacks and the coloureds were kicked and hit and then hit again just wherever they could lay a baton on them.

There were screaming, frightened people all around me and yet I knew I could get away if I really wanted to. All I had to do was make a fuss. I could tell them I was going to report them. I could say I would get a lawyer involved. I could demand and I could threaten. There was no end to the things I could do because I was white, and I knew that if I did, within a very few minutes they would let me go – but I didn't do any of them.

I thought, no. They wanted me and now they've got me and I'm going to go all the way with this. The whole thing was just so totally disgusting.

Through the wire mesh around the vans I could see Leon Markowitz, who was then Mayor of Cape Town and whom I happened to know, running down the road. He had come to see what was going on. I hung onto the inside of the wire and called out to him.

I called him loudly by his name. 'Leon,' I shouted. 'Please tell Kobus. Tell him you saw me. Tell him where I am.' My father was overseas at the time.

Then he was gone and I was alone and when you're alone like that you become very frightened. There were terrible stories in those days. People disappeared and were never heard of again. The police, the government could do anything they liked and get away with it. It seemed to us then there was no one who could stop them. I thought about my children. I thought about the irresponsibility of doing what I'd done, but I thought about the incomparably greater amount that so many others had done and were doing, much of which we were only to learn about later after the change of government came about.

There were a very great many of us and we were all taken to the main police station at Caledon Square to be charged. I'm not quite sure what we were going to be charged with, but we were going to be charged. And we were all purple from head to toe. Kobus told me afterwards that the only things about me that weren't purple were the whites of my eyes. Even my earrings were purple. (Kobus described it all very nicely when we appeared in court afterwards.)

I remember the human rights lawyers coming and saying it was all right, that everything had been sorted out.

While I was at Caledon Square waiting for the 'sort out' I remember one policeman looking at me and saying: '*Maar jy's mos*

Prof. Barnard se dogter, jy't most gewaterski. You're Prof. Barnard's daughter, you used to waterski.'

I said, 'Ja.'

He said, '*Jy was so dik, nou is jy so dun.* You were so fat, and now you're so thin.'

We stayed there until midnight. A special court was set up and we were let off on our own recognisance and had to promise never to take part in a march again.

It didn't seem very long afterwards that FW de Klerk, who was then State President (and then-husband of our one-outfit-only client, Marike) publicly announced that he was beginning the process that would lead to the scrapping of apartheid and the change of government.

11

While we're on the subject

*The story of someone my father
considered a truly remarkable man*

My father was not Top of the Pops with absolutely everyone. His prima donna temperament has often been referred to. His last wife, Karin, when she wrote about the Chris Barnard she knew, probably summed it up very well when she said:

> He is an absolute perfectionist. He has great determination and a very strong will, and a big sense of achievement. There is nothing or nobody that will stop him from doing something he really wants to do.
>
> He does have some bad characteristics, of course – after all, he is only human! He has absolutely no patience, and indeed, the word doesn't even exist in his vocabulary. He is also very impulsive and sometimes gets himself into trouble by acting on the spur of the moment. He loses his temper too quickly, sometimes about very minor things. Tact is also a quality he does not have in any great abundance and he tends to say things irrespective of the consequences.

My father was fully aware that all three of his wives felt the same way about him.

'As a matter of fact,' he said, 'all three of my wives are of the same opinion. I am a moody, selfish, irritable perfectionist. I am never wrong and modesty isn't my strong point. But apart from that I'm really quite a nice guy.'

As I re-read the above I'm rather afraid that much the same kind of thing is going to pop up in my own obituary one day. Except, I hope, for the part about the temper!

In any case, he had his faults. A nursing sister who phoned in to a radio programme said she'd worked with him and that he was a 'pig'. Let's hope he was at least a 'pig' in a good cause!

I also got fed up with him sometimes. I am not a full-time Miss Goody Two Shoes. I loved my father but I'd have to be pretty blinkered if I pretended he didn't have two sides and that Karin and the nurse didn't sum up his irritable side fairly accurately.

The last child who came to South Africa as a beneficiary of funding from the Christiaan Barnard Foundation was a little boy from Russia. Susan Vosloo, a wonderful paediatric heart surgeon and an extremely nice person, was going to do the operation. My father travelled on the same plane as the mother and baby.

I must say here what I'll probably say again before I finish, which is how much my father loved children. He would always single the children out of a crowd and go over and have a word with them.

He always said the implantation of a heart valve in a child is a most difficult task for any surgeon. It's more difficult than doing it in an adult and it's often a challenge abandoned by even the most capable surgeons.

In those days, before arthritis prevented him from doing the operating himself, performing heart surgery on children was a task my father would undertake when others would not. I think it showed very clearly the two traits that dominated his character. He was willing to face a challenge and he always believed that children had a right to every opportunity life could afford them, which is something I endorse and believe in absolutely myself.

My father was not the tidiest person in the world. His office, especially in those last days when he was on his own with no one to 'supervise' him, was extremely untidy.

After the operation on the little Russian boy, which had been a great success, he was on his way to a press conference and there was something he wanted to take with him. He'd had a fax from Mikhail Gorbachev, extending his warmest wishes and thanking the Christiaan Barnard Foundation for choosing a Russian boy to give this life-changing operation to.

He couldn't find the fax anywhere, which to the untutored eye would not be all that surprising. He was flipping through papers, muttering angrily because he was expected shortly at the press conference and a big reception at the then City Park Hospital (now the Christiaan Barnard Memorial Hospital).

'*Waar's die donnerse faks?*' he demanded. 'Where's the bloody fax?'

I told him to calm down, but I knew him when he was like this. The smaller the irritant, the more irritated he got, until eventually he was thundering around, very cross with himself and with anyone who happened to be in his path.

I found the fax and gave it to him. It was very complimentary. It said:

> Dear friend! I am happy to know about this successful surgery and recovery of the little Russian boy. This saved life and returned happiness to the family are possible only because of your generosity and nobility, the high professionalism of the doctors of your clinic and the effectiveness of your assistants from your Foundation. We are sincerely grateful to you and proud of you. Hope to continue our

co-operation and to see you soon. Gratefully, Mikhail Gorbachev.

There may have been a 'gratefully' from Mikhail Gorbachev, but you know how it is in those situations. There was not going to be a 'gratefully', never mind a 'thank you' for me for finding the fax. What there was going to be was some more thundering. Then the piece about how we'd better get a move on if we wanted to get to the press conference in time, as if the whole world had to snap to attention because there was something that Prof. had to do. How can you possibly stop yourself getting irritated with a man who behaves like this?

'You know what you are?' I said. 'You are a spoilt brat.'

I was not in the habit of talking to my father like this. I tend always to let things go. Not just with him but with everyone, but it was one of those times again when something in you just rises up and says enough is enough.

He was huffy, I was huffy. We left for the press conference and we were a bit stiff and formal with each other for a while, and a bit cold-shouldered, and then things moved on. The Russian boy was discharged from hospital. My father said a few words. The fax was displayed and the incident forgotten. Or, at least I thought it had been.

Some time later – with no thought of this at all in my mind – I phoned my father, as I sometimes did, to ask him a medical question. A friend's mother had Alzheimer's. What information could I pass on to her, saying, 'My dad said so'?

My father was always very good about things like this. Clearly Alzheimer's was not his speciality but he always kept up to date on what was happening in all facets of his profession. He was also very willing to put things into layperson's terms where he could and to help people. He knew very well that these informal questions were put to him not in the expectation of a formal diagnosis but simply by people seeking some kind of reassurance.

He told me what he could about that particular condition. He also gave me a few words of comfort and advice to give to my friend and then he finished the conversation by saying (I'm sorry to tell you, rather triumphantly): 'That's all I know. That's all a spoilt brat can do to help you now.'

My remark had clearly hit home. Equally clearly, he couldn't resist getting in the last word.

⁓

This was one side of my father. There was another side also. When I was at school, we had an outing to the University of Cape Town's Medical School at Groote Schuur to see what my father did. It was a kind of field trip and he was very happy to introduce the party of schoolgirls to some aspects of hospital life. I was quite pleased with myself. I suppose it's my old wanting-to-be accepted thing. In any case, it was like everything else in life. Which is to say it was good and it was bad too.

It was good because my father and his staff went to a lot of trouble to make it interesting for us. It was bad because the slides he'd prepared showing some aspects of the work they were doing at Groote Schuur made some of the girls faint and everyone felt sorry for the animals that were used in research.

I know this is a thorny issue. I imagine some of you reading this might feel just as squeamish about laboratory animals as those girls from Standard 3 at Rustenburg Junior School did, and of course we're all at liberty to respond to testing on animals in any way we think appropriate.

The reality is that in those days animals were used for research and there were people who took care of them. There were two assistants in the animal laboratory. Both of them were black men. One was called Hamilton Naki and the other Frederick Snyders, but he was known as Boots, probably because of the huge, white lab boots they used to wear.

I sometimes used to go back to the lab if I happened to be in the area, just to say hullo. One day when I got there I was told that Boots had died. Poor Boots, I kept remembering how he'd had to cope with all those fainting people on that day long ago, the squeamish little white girls from the Standard 3 class at Rustenburg Junior School.

Boots and Hamilton were both very nice, extremely helpful men, but Hamilton was very particular about his work. His name was mentioned very often in our house along with the names of those other members of the team who worked with my father.

My father's old friend, the film-maker Dirk de Villiers, is working with Hamilton at the moment on a film about his life due to be screened on SATV. If you want to see a story about a remarkable man then you'd better watch out for this movie, but I'd like to tell you just a little bit about Hamilton here, and not because it vaunts my father in any way. Hamilton's life and achievements are his own. I want to tell his story simply because references to Hamilton were a part of the day-to-day talk in my early life and because my father so much admired him. I have talked about his lack of patience and his low frustration threshold. It was true on a domestic level but it was true at another, much higher and more important level also.

If my father was angry and frustrated that children should be born into this world imperfect, with heart defects – which he was – you should also know how great his frustration was that so many people of potential ability in this country were fettered because of their race.

Hamilton was born in the village of Ngcingane in the rural area of Centane in what was then known as Transkei. He was educated to high school level and in 1940 he came to Cape Town looking for work. He got a job as a gardener at the University of Cape Town. Fourteen years later he was transferred to a cleaning position at Medical School, where Robert Goetz, a German professor who was conducting vascular research, came across him.

The Medical School needed to use all its resources to maximum effect because of its limited funding and this German professor decided to take Hamilton on as his assistant.

With no formal training, Hamilton began anaesthetising and preparing the animals to be used in research. Then, when it was clear that he had abilities, he began performing the operations himself.

My father and all those many others working in his field were quick to acknowledge how important the 'backroom' laboratory work was. Without it, the odds against an even partly guaranteed end result would have been impossible.

Hamilton was amazingly thorough and adept at what he did. Everyone who saw his work admired his skills. Dr Rose Hickman, a renowned surgeon herself, said in a television documentary screened in 1992 that Hamilton was absolutely dedicated to his work and had that 'indefinable quality' that makes a fine surgeon.

My father said that Hamilton was more skilled than many of the junior doctors and was 'quite capable' of performing heart surgery on a human being. In fact, he said: 'He could perform heart transplants and liver transplants, which are very complicated. I could not do liver transplants. He had more skill than I have on the technical side.'

'The arrival of Professor Chris Barnard in 1956 was a blessing in disguise for me,' Hamilton told a local newspaper recently, 'because we were always performing transplants together as he was responsible for cardiac research.'

Yet, during those apartheid years, Hamilton was not permitted even to stand beside my father in the operating theatre.

Hamilton was an incredibly neat and dapper dresser and an extremely dignified and upright man. His tie was always straight and beautifully knotted and his shoes gleamed. This pride in his appearance reflected his perfectionist attitude to his work. 'Everything he did, he did well,' said my father.

My father, although I am quite sure he wouldn't have said anything about Hamilton's attitude to his appearance, would certainly have approved. Like Hamilton, he was always neat and tidy and liked to dress appropriately for an occasion. In his later life, when he could afford it, he was always extremely well tailored. Vanity, you might say, and you might be right, but it went rather deeper than that. It was something he spoke about once to a group of students at Medunsa University, the medical school set up for aspiring black doctors who were denied access to the white universities in the days of apartheid.

The dress code at the university was extremely casual. I don't think my father would have minded that. In the nature of things, students tend to be casual, but what was good for a student was not necessarily good for a practising doctor. When practitioners respect their profession, they dress accordingly. That was my father's view. You don't go waterskiing in a dinner suit unless you're a clown in a water pageant and you don't make a patient visit unless you are properly and soberly dressed. (Which explains why he had a superb collection of ties – but we'll return to that at the end of the chapter.) That was the view of his time. It was a view that suited Hamilton and my father perfectly.

Hamilton is retired now, but during his 42-year professional life he helped to train a generation of young doctors.

'People don't believe it now,' Hamilton says. 'An uneducated person training those with degrees.'

But he did. He taught more than 3 000 trainee doctors and retired after all those years of service on a gardener's pension. As a token of appreciation he was given a water jug. That was his retirement present! 'I still have that water jug at home,' he says. 'My wife wanted to die when she saw that present.'

When my father retired he too was given a gift 'for 25 years' faithful service'. Possibly in the grip of hubris, he thought he was going to be given a Rolex watch. The size of the parcel and the way it was wrapped gave a hint that it might be, but it wasn't.

My father's retirement gift was a hospital necktie with a laundry instruction attached that declared it to be washable. I can just imagine what Hamilton's wife must have felt.

While he was working at Medical School, Hamilton lived in a single sex hostel in Langa, a township outside Cape Town. His family remained in the Transkei and he would see them once a year when he went on his annual holiday. Hamilton, on his gardener's salary, supported 24 people.

In the later years my father's own rise to fame was used in a television advert with the strap line 'Search for the hero inside yourself.' In the advertisement a few famous South African life stories were singled out as an example to young people. Unlike the few people in the ad, Hamilton is one of so many examples of unfulfilled potential – just one among so many who were held back, their abilities curbed by the restrictive policies of the Nationalist government. One cannot give one single one of them their life to start over, but Hamilton's approach to life is nevertheless a positive one.

He says what is important is the foundation he's laid. 'Not all young people can go to universities or technikons, but all of them have talent of one kind or another.' In an effort to ensure that this talent is recognised and developed, Hamilton has started a fund to help children who can't get an education because of financial problems. 'What happened to me must not happen to others.' That is his view and he is doing something positive about it. Something that will give some young person the chances he never had.

In later life, Hamilton finally received the recognition due to him. He is to receive an honour in Langa, where he still lives. He is also to be honoured by the provincial government of the Eastern Cape, where he was born, for the lifetime of work he did training young doctors and also for the role he played in that first historic heart transplant. In 2002 the South African government awarded him the new Order of Mapungubwe, and in 2003 the University of Cape Town gave him an honorary doctorate.

I see his composed, dignified figure before me as I write and in my photograph album I have a picture of Hamilton in a surgeon's mask and gown at work on one of his operations.

He is a very special man and an inspiration in his own way, and I hope the film that is being made about him is well and widely received and brings the invaluable role he played to the wider audience it deserves.

But now, finally, to the Matter of My Father's Neck-Ties.

I have discovered Camp Joy. It's not a Baptist revival centre and it's not a holiday farm for gay boys either. It's a new project for street children here in Cape Town that I have recently got involved in. Everyone who knows me knows about me and children, and I have just met someone new. His name is Jermaine and he's very proud of his appearance. He has a red cardboard suitcase he keeps under his bunk bed. When I went to Camp Joy we struck up a friendship and he offered to show me his things in the way friends do. He pulled out his suitcase from under the bed and showed me his prize possessions. He has a photograph of a man wearing a tie. I do not know who this man is and he didn't tell me. He has Nugget shoe polish to polish his shoes and he has two face-cloths, one to wash his face and one for his *boude*, his buttocks.

Just think about your own life and the children in your life and then stop for a moment and think about that.

I sat on that bunk bed and looked at the items from that red suitcase set out before me and I started to cry. You know, when my publishers read the first draft of this book they said to me that I can't always have been so happy about everything, and that's true. They said it's all right if I want to tell some of the sad stuff too, and I know that they're right, and so I have.

My father cried when things moved him and sometimes they were what might seem like small things. A song like 'Skipskop', for instance, he cried every time he heard that, although it's about a very different thing, the forced removal of a fishing village, the disintegration of a community and the irretrievable loss inherent in that. As he grew older, and I sat quietly in his living room with him, watching him weep as he listened and weeping with him, it seemed to me that my father wept not only for the sadness of all that had happened in his own country, which he loved dearly. I believe he also saw elements of his life in David Kramer's poignant words:

'n stukkie lê hier	(A piece here
en 'n stukkie lê daar	A piece there
die stukkies van my lewe	The pieces of my life
hulle lê deurmekaar	Lie everywhere)

Sometimes it's just life with all its little ironies and sometimes it's the big things, like the time when Barbara died and the break-up of the last little family. He certainly cried then. I know it's all right to cry and I've cried too, plenty of times. As you get older you learn that there's more than enough going on in the world that could make you weep and when you think of this, those things that have happened in your own life seem very small by comparison.

I cried at Camp Joy. I sat on that bed and saw that young boy, Jermaine, with all of his life still ahead of him and all of that hope in his face and there I was doing the crying number. Tears, by the way, are a big attention-catcher, just when you need least of all to be looked at, so there were all the other boys looking at me, this woman sitting on a bed all *snot en trane*, with her eyes and nose streaming, as if she'd lost her marbles.

In any case, I made up my mind about something. I thought

about the man in Jermaine's photograph, so neat in his tie, and how Jermaine told me that they have their Nugget and face-cloths but no ties for church.

My father, who liked to dress in an *ordentlike*, proper way, had ties. I had been keeping them, treasuring them really, and they were in my house all neat and tidy in mothballs. Well, they are out of mothballs now and each boy at Camp Joy has one and it's better that way and I cried some more because of it. Not because of parting with my father's ties, although they were precious to me, but because of Jermaine. Jermaine is a boy who greets you with a sturdy handshake, his shoes shine with Nugget and he can now go to church in a tie from Harrods once owned by a man who'd have known what it was I was crying about.

You may begin with very little but you have to start somewhere and Jermaine has the 'look' and the 'attitude' and ... *so 'n man kan ver in die lewe vorder* ... a man like that can go far in life.

12

Love and loss

'Grief is pain beyond description.'
[My father]
'My father was absolutely right.'
[Me]

My father died in Paphos, Crete, on Sunday 2 September 2001. He'd been on a working visit to Israel to see for himself the impact of some of the latest technology on medical research. He was very excited about it.

The Cretan visit was meant to have been a holiday. My father loved Crete. Among the many honours bestowed on him was the gift of Greek citizenship, and this was given to him by a unanimous vote of the Greek parliament. The Greeks are passionate people. They love their country. They don't offer citizenship to every person they see on the street. To honour someone with the gift of their citizenship in this way is no small thing; it's the greatest measure of esteem they can offer. My father knew this very well and because he knew it he valued it greatly.

The irony, which was not lost on my father, was that if he'd been born a Cretan he would probably never have been in business as a heart surgeon at all, because the diseases my father specialised in are virtually unknown on the island of Crete thanks to their healthy Mediterranean diet.

My father had been happy in Crete before and I hoped he would be happy again. He was tired. On the outside he put on a good show of being his usual ebullient self, but inside he was worn out. I felt it. He was unused to being alone: he liked people around him and he loved home life. He was used to a house where there were children: he missed Armin and Lara. This was the third family he'd lost. There are some who might say that in a sense my father managed to self-sabotage, to destroy all those things that were precious to him, and perhaps there's an element of truth in this. The fact is that the moment when it happens, whatever the causes may have been, the pain is real enough.

When I think about it now it seems to me I'd begun grieving for him at the moment it became clear that his last marriage wasn't working out and that when it formally ended he would be entering a new, far more solitary phase of his life. It was a bad time for him. He had once written that there can be no more saddening experience than to sit in a divorce court and watch the legal process dissolve years of commitment in a few minutes.

My father was sad. It hurt me to see it; his sadness deep-etched itself into me. He had not been well: there had been the disfiguring cancer of the nose; he'd had a hip replacement; and the relentless pain of arthritis, like his asthma, was always with him. I couldn't bear to see him so alone and in such distress. When I was in my final year at school and my mother told me she and my father were getting a divorce, my first response was to ask, if this indeed had to happen, who would there be to take care of my father.

It was a question I now asked myself again. If I were to be the one to care for him I would have been quite content, but I knew I was already fussing too much and worrying too much. I knew that I couldn't fill the void that had opened up in his life.

It's a shame to have to own up to this, but sometimes my poor father would just have to sit quietly and listen politely while I tried to push him in some direction I wanted him to go, where he had no intention of going at all. But then, what works for one person doesn't always work for another.

I kept telephoning people he knew, urging them to visit him and cheer him up. I went out and collected brochures for fantastic cruises. I pressed things on him that he really didn't want at all and he suffered it with great forbearance. In fact, considering all the things his wives and the other people who knew said about my father and how temperamental he could be, he suffered it all very patiently indeed.

He sat in his town house listening to Kris Kristoffersen singing 'Lover Come Back'. It's funny, in a way, I suppose. Noël Coward was right when he said how potent cheap music can be, and there's bathos in the picture of a lovelorn man, no longer young, listening to a sentimental song about love and about loss – but it's sad too. I suppose you can't help but wonder if, after all, this is what all the glitter and stardust amounted to in the end.

There was a memorial service for my father in the Cape Town City Hall. It's a beautiful old building with all kinds of memories attached to it. It was from a balcony of this same City Hall that Nelson Mandela made his address to the world after his release from Victor Verster prison in February 1990.

There were a great many people there from all walks of life. It made me feel very small. All these people who had come to honour my father and say goodbye to him, who came over to our family and offered their few words of comfort and sometimes their thanks, to acknowledge our loss.

Why is it that a huge mass of people are called a 'sea'? I suppose because it really is like that, all of us bobbing along side by side in our small lives and then something considered important in the greater community happens and people flock together and acknowledge it.

That's how it was in that old building on that day. The life of the city went on outside. It was business as usual on the Grand Parade, parking for most people was a problem, the informal parking attendants were as full of lip as ever, cars shot the traffic lights they way they always do. The air was full of the smell of life being lived and the fish and chips being fried in the Grand Parade fish and chip shop.

The world didn't stand still. There were no 'crape bows round the white necks of the public doves' (in WH Andrew's now famous words), but for a moment there was a pause and in that pause Anneli Cilliers sang 'Skipskop', that sad song my father was so fond of.

But it was over now, the revels ended, the glamour, the clamour, the glory and the pain. I remembered (and this is an anecdote I'll return to later) Dr Denton Cooley's joking welcome to my father when he greeted him in Houston in those halcyon days that seem so long ago. 'Hi, boy!' he said. 'What's your name?'

That's what it all came down to in the end.

My own view is that his new life – as a man on his own, without Karin and the little family he loved so much and missed such a very great deal – would not have been the life he would have chosen for himself – no matter how brave a face he showed the world, or how often he reminded me, sometimes rather tartly, that he had a life of his own which I had to respect in just the same way he respected my life.

He could be very droll about it. Sometimes when I was fussing around my son, Tiaan, who suffered it in much the same way my father did, Tiaan would mutter how he'd wished he'd stayed in university residence where at least his life was his own and he wouldn't have me clucking around him.

My father, I think, was sympathetic towards him. He often

quoted Tiaan to himself and after a particularly obvious dose of fussing he'd say rather sagely: 'You see, Tiaan, don't you wish now you'd stayed in university residence instead of coming home?'

But even when he was trying his hardest to put on a brave face, something in my father was broken. I could feel it.

At this time of my father's life, while I was dropping hints that were about as subtle as putting something on a Breaking News story on CNN, I kept suggesting he should maybe go on a cruise or find himself some new little number. 'Little number' is a catchphrase of mine. I use it for clothes and I use it for young women. My father had used to find it amusing but he wasn't in a frame of mind to be amused by it now. Things were going on in my father's life that he couldn't be jollied out of, that no cruise ship in the world could have fixed. Perhaps I shouldn't even have suggested it.

Of course, I realise life is not really that simple. It's just that at times in my life, getting on a liner and going off into the blue, leaving the real world behind me, really did something wonderful for me. As I've already mentioned, I wanted him to take his good friend Maureen Brink on a round-the-world cruise on the *QE2*. I enthused about it to my father. I cracked all those silly jokes about how Maureen could be his fourth wife and look after him. He listened with his usual attention, but all the enthusiasm was on my side.

It's a very hard thing not to have the tools that can make someone you love better. I felt my lack of them then and it hurt me.

I didn't expect my father to die. That sounds a very obvious statement, but all platitudes turn out to be right in the end. Anyone can die at any time. My father was far from being in his dotage, but he was no longer a young man. When our parents begin to get visibly older, I suppose that somewhere, deep inside ourselves, we should all begin to prepare ourselves for that time when they'll leave us, although even as I write this down I realise what nonsense it is.

Nothing prepares us for death, even in the old, and certainly not for a death that was not preceded by illness and happened as far from home as his death did.

~

This is how I heard about it.

I was with my mother, our good friend Dene and my husband, Kobus. We were driving out of Cape Town on the West Coast road that goes along the coastline to Saldanha Bay. It travels along windblown scrubland on one side. On the other side is the Atlantic Ocean. The further you get from Cape Town, the simpler life becomes. All you see as you drive along this national road is signboards for Melkbosstrand, Mamre, Kreeftebaai, Malmesbury, Darling, Philadelphia, Moorreesburg.

I know these places. I know the people there and they are the kind of people I like. For the most part they're good, honest people. Their word alone is good enough to seal any bargain. They are as dependable as the land that sustains them. They are the kind of people my father, always so proud of his small town roots, liked too.

We were on our way to the funeral of our old friend Auntie Rita van Rooyen. My mother had treated us to a wonderful breakfast (the food thing again!). If my father had been in the country he would have been with us, for in their later years my parents had resumed contact, as I'll discuss later. Auntie Rita and Oom Hentie were the owners of Hentie's Botel on the Knysna Lakes at which my parents had given my brother Andre and me the best family holidays and on which I'd first learnt to waterski.

All the memories of our time together with Auntie Rita and her late husband were of long summer days spent completely at ease, of laughter and the undemanding companionship of people of similar spirit who give much and ask little. In some deep part of myself the memories of those laughter-filled days were embedded along with all my happiest recollections.

As we drove along that day, my life was the same as it is every day. Everything was in its rightful place in my memory bank, just like it always is, and then the mobile phone rang.

I am not one for mobile telephones. I, even I, sometimes like peace and quiet. I like to talk but I don't like disturbing other people in public places with my chatter, and also I'm jumpy about everyone talking to everyone else on mobile phones because it's so nice when you're doing it and then it's so terrible when the bills start arriving.

My father had firm views about mobile phones. In his book *Fifty Ways to a Healthy Heart* (highly recommended by at least one satisfied reader I know) he has a whole chapter called 'Tame Your Mobile Phone'. He was always interested in new things but he thought that too much technology could only end up cluttering your life. Once you let technology in at the front door, if you didn't watch out it could take over to such an extent you might forget what it was to be human.

Machines cannot give love, my father said. So we should watch out for them, because love can heal a great many things far beyond the skills of any doctor this world has yet seen.

People who knew my father knew that once, when Karin had a mobile that gave up the ghost, he used to carry it around with him as a prop. When he saw a potentially boring situation coming his way he used to take the phone out and pretend to be talking, knowing that he could wander politely out of harm's way still holding the phone.

But even my father came to realise that mobiles have their uses. When he was away he gave his mobile to me, so we could keep in touch with each other. I think he did it for my sake, to please me, as much as for himself.

I couldn't bear the idea that my father might feel lonely. He always said he didn't. The trouble is, I didn't know if I could trust him to tell me the truth. The one thing I know is that in families we sometimes say things not because they're what we truly feel but because we think they're the things the other person needs to hear. We do it because we love them.

And here are some examples of what I mean.

If I asked my mother, in those days, if she minded – if it would hurt her – if I went to spend some time with my father and Barbara, she would say no. She would say, of course I must go. She would say that whatever I chose to do would be perfectly fine with her.

If I asked my father please to phone me at any hour of the day or night, to come to my house – which was a home for him too whenever he needed it, especially after the last divorce – he would say we must respect each other's privacy. I have a husband. I have children and a family life that is dear to me, and he wouldn't encroach on that.

He would say, quite sternly, that he had a life too. He knew that I meant well, but he was quite capable of looking after himself. The last thing he needed was an anxious daughter forever on the doorstep, checking that the house was in order, whether the cupboards were full, wanting to make tea or see that he was eating properly.

For people who have so much to say and pride themselves on being frank or in many cases just plain outspoken, I am not all that sure that the Barnards are such good communicators as they may seem to be at first glance; but I will come to that later.

For now it's enough to say that I am still the one who has my father's mobile, even if I am always a bit scared about using it, because for me every time I dial a number on a mobile phone, what I see in my head is the slot machines at Sun City. You pour lots of money into them and unless you're really lucky that's the last time you see it. I know because I once worked for Sol Kerzner, the hotel magnate and Sun King himself. At least at his places you got something back. You could win the jackpot or even a motor car.

I liked to talk to my father. From Crete he phoned me to tell me how the trip was going. He phoned me at the hairdresser to ask for the rugby score, but we couldn't talk properly because the line wasn't good, so I had to phone back and just for a change I let the slot machine pictures take care of themselves and we had a really nice long talk.

He was all right. The trip was going well. We talked about a great many things and I went to bed happy, and I know something now I didn't know before. My father was wrong. Machines may not be able to give love directly but they can certainly play a role in making you feel loved and reassured. They can make you feel better for having spoken to someone you care about: in other words, they can be a lifeline. I would not have missed that call or made it one second shorter, not for anything in the world.

On the Sunday, when the phone rang, I thought it was Pappa. It was the kind of thing he did. Auntie Rita had been his friend. Our families had all been friends together over very many years. If he hadn't been away he would definitely have been with us to pay his last respects. He would have wanted us to tell Auntie Rita's daughters, Reinet and Elna, that he'd called, that he sent his love, that he was sad not to be there and was thinking of us. My father was like that. His friends were important to him. In the ups and downs of their lives, in good times or bad, he liked to be there to share in celebrations and offer support in adversity.

But it wasn't my father on the telephone. It was a quarter to one. It was Sunday afternoon on that road between the wind-stunted, bush-covered sand dunes on the one side and the full roll of the Atlantic Ocean on the other. We were just outside the fishing town of Saldanha Bay, the place where the funeral was to be held, and the call was from my father's friend Costas. He was phoning from the Coral Beach Hotel in Paphos.

He said: 'Deirdre, I am sorry, but I have very bad news for you
...' And that was the start of it: the start of my life without my
father.

Kobus pulled the car to the side of the road and I cried. I did-
n't know I could cry like that. I didn't know I had so many tears
in me.

In the days of my waterskiing, when we lived by the lake – on
those bad days when it was still dark, those days of making myself
wake up, knowing that I had to get up on my skis and out on the
ice cold water – I used to cry. I cried out of frustration because I
knew this is what I would have to do if I wanted to succeed. I cried
because I wanted more than anything for someone to come along
and tell me there was some short-cut, easier way to do it.
Preferably one that would make it possible for me to lie under my
nice warm blankets for a little while longer, the way other girls
were doing. The trouble is that there is no short cut. You can cry
just as hard and as long as you like, but there are certain things in
life that have to be done the hard way because there is no other
way. If I hadn't known it before, I certainly knew it now. There is
no short cut.

As I've already told you, my mother, who had her own ideas
about these things, used to say at least half the water in the lake
was made up of my tears. But I knew nothing of weeping until
that day, in that place, when I took that phone call from Crete,
from my father's friend Costas, who told me my father had died.

It must have been hard for him to be the one to do it. I realise
that now. There's no good way to tell someone something like this.
Costas is a nice man. I think he knew that those few seconds while
the phone was ringing, while I was scratching around trying to
find it, were my last few seconds of being the woman I'd been.
After that, once I'd answered, once he'd said what he had to say,
nothing could ever be quite the same for me again. I think it took
courage for him to be the one to tell me.

My father said that grief is pain beyond description. He was right. He said it was a pain so unbearable there had to be some special word to describe it because the word 'pain' by itself just wasn't big enough. He was right about that too.

My mother knows grief and my mother is a remarkable woman. My brother, so close to me in age that for one month of the year we were the same age, had died. People say that the worst grief is for a parent to lose a child because such a loss confounds the natural order of things. Parents are meant to die before their children.

My mother certainly knew grief when my brother died, and my father too. I grieved for my brother in my way, but my way was different from that of my parents. I was sad because my brother died young. He had a good wife and lovely children. He was a talented and capable man who still had much to offer in life, who should have lived to see his children grow up, who should have grown old. I was sad, I think, because of the days that were denied him, but at that time I did not know grief.

My knowledge of grief was my father's last gift to me. Perhaps you think 'gift' is a strange word, but it isn't, because I have learnt something now, a life lesson I didn't know before. At least now when someone suffers loss I know enough not to say, 'I know how you feel'. People so often say that, especially in the face of loss. I am surprised that they dare to.

13

The Full Catastrophe

'Am I married? Am I not a man and is a man
not married? Of course I'm married.
A wife, a house, children, the full catastrophe.'
[The film version of Nikos Kazantzakis's
wonderful book *Zorba the Greek*]

We went to Auntie Rita's funeral. No turning back, that's what we
agreed. We had to go on to the funeral. Our friends were expecting us, but for me the simple phrase 'no turning back' had a far
greater significance than that.

I was driving along that road with all the pieces of my life in
that same place they always were, and then suddenly everything
was changed. My father was gone from me. He was gone from us
all. There was a time when he had seemed to me to be indestruc-
tible, but now he had entered the past.

It's funny how a small thing can be such a hard thing, but it's a
very hard to thing to begin that process in which you learn to
speak and to think about someone so close to you in the past
tense. It is so strange. You do it in one sentence. *'Pappa is dood.*
Dadda is dead.' I am going to have to say this to Oom Hentie and
his daughters and all those others whom I know and that is the last
time I will ever speak of my father in the present tense. It is like
standing on the quayside while a great ship like the *Oriana* slides

away on one of her journeys and you stand there waving and watching as the ship gets smaller and smaller until it finally disappears. It is one of the saddest, loneliest feelings in the world, but when it comes to you, you know immediately what it is. Even so I was lucky. I've thought about it since and decided that God was good to me.

Our friends had their grief too and in a way it was wonderful that fate had seen fit to bring us all together in this way in that place on that day.

My wonderful husband Kobus was there. (I really think one day someone must give Kobus a medal for always being there for the Barnard family just when we need him most, and always knowing the right thing to do and the right words to say.)

And my mother was there. I can't imagine my mother not having been there. In his last interview with *Time* magazine my father said of my mother:

'All the credit must go to Louwtjie, my first wife, who took the strain and stood by me when we were young. She married me because she loved me.'

She did, and I don't know what things were in my mother's heart on that day. She and my father had walked a long, bumpy road together, and now that walk too was ended.

My mother married my father for better or worse, in church, in the sight of God, and my mother is steadfast and a woman of her word. When she commits to something, for her it is a total commitment. She bore my father his first two children, my brother Andre and me. She made his first family and she stood at the heart of it. She was a wonderful daughter-in-law to his parents and nothing was ever to damage that special relationship she had with them.

I think that in the early years they had their good times. My father always said how much he loved the time he spent in general practice at Ceres. That was where he and my mother stayed in the early days of their married life when he was a GP. He said afterwards that he'd left the Ceres practice only because it couldn't support three partners.

He'd had an opportunity to take up a scholarship in London, but had turned it down because he didn't want to leave his young family. It's ironic, I suppose, but on the other hand it's exactly how life is.

If he'd taken up that scholarship it's almost certain his life would have been very different. It's unlikely that he would ever have gone to Minneapolis or that all that came after would have happened to him, and if his life had been different I imagine our lives would have been different too, but it didn't happen that way. Of course after the transplant, when life changed for us all, it was my mother who bore the brunt of that change.

She must have had her memories that day when we sat by the roadside and considered our sad news. My mother knew sad news and she knew loss. She knew things she couldn't possibly have imagined when she was a young theatre sister from Okahandja being courted by a newly qualified doctor from Beaufort West. My mother has had quite a life. Now the life she had set out on with my father had come a full 360 degrees.

Towards the end, they began to spend time together. The old sparks of attraction between them were still there and in their old age they formed an uneasy, potentially volcanic alliance.

The last function my father attended in South Africa was a fundraising dinner for the Organ Donor Foundation of Southern Africa. It was the day before he left for Israel on the first leg of a journey that was to be the last from his own country.

He was guest speaker and he looked very fine. My mother had shortened the trousers of the new dinner suit he wore. He seemed to enjoy telling people this. I suppose in a way it was like coming full circle, all the way from those long-ago days when she had fine-stitched those heart valves for him in that time of their young married life. It was during the time when Andre and I were small and she used to make our clothes. We were a long way from the high life in those days and she also sewed to earn extra money.

On that night, which was to be his last 'big night out', my father seemed extremely taken by what my mother had done for him. Not only had she turned out her usual perfect work, she'd done it without his even having to try the pants on, and the end result could have held its own with the best tailoring anywhere.

I suppose there's some irony in the fact that having sacrificed so much for him, and despite all that had passed between them, at the end my mother was still performing small, almost wifely services for my father.

My mother, I think, would be impatient with this view of things because far too much had happened in the interim to leave any room for sentimentality. I suppose one could have speculated how else their tempestuous journey might finally have ended. It could so easily have been with a firework display of temperament that would gave rivalled the River of Fire over the Thames on Millennium night. They were perfectly capable of that too, but it didn't happen.

The truth is that the journey of my mother, Aletta Louw, who married her freshly qualified country doctor in 1948, didn't end in a shower of fire. It ended on a small domestic note, something which, I am sure, neither of them could ever have imagined all that long time ago when they first met.

I cannot know what she felt. What I know is that when I heard of my father's death I wanted my mother, and I think it is the same for anyone lucky enough to have a good mother. It's nice to share joys with your mother, but when something goes wrong it's always our mother we turn to first if she's there, and miss most if she isn't, and there she was just the same way she'd always been.

It was important that our old friend Dene was there. I think

Dene has been there for just about every big thing that ever happened in our family. Dene and her family have been great friends of ours. She became my father's secretary and when she got drawn into his world she became a medical technologist, a perfusionist who operates the essential support machine while an operation is taking place. But our shared history goes well back to Zeekoevlei days.

When Dene's father – Captain, as he was known, of the Zeekoevlei Power Boat Club down at our home lake – was diagnosed with lung cancer, my father was truly devastated. He told her he hadn't slept all night after he heard the news, thinking about what was going to happen.

My father always said he never minded standing on any toes, official or otherwise, if it served a good purpose. When Dene's father was diagnosed, my father went out of his way to get permission from the medical authorities to import a new drug from America that had not yet been cleared for medical use. He had it flown out to South Africa and he told Dene and her family that he was using it experimentally. It was the best he could do. He had nothing else to offer. Unfortunately, there was to be no reprieve despite my father's efforts, and Captain died and we shared her loss. Now she was there to share ours.

It was a strange day, but if that was meant to be the time and the place where I had first to face up to the fact that my father was no longer in this world, then that was the way of it. Even so, because my Kobus, my mother and Dene were with me, I was blessed.

When we arrived in Saldanha Bay at the funeral I think it was clear to others just by looking at us that something had happened, and because the people who were waiting for us were the kind of people they are, it was easy to tell them. It was easy to cry in front of them.

Grief is often a private thing. For some it's an ugly thing to see and for some, embarrassing. People turn away or say things that are meant to deflect the feelings, and I understand that. Seeing someone grieving is to see them exposed. I suppose it makes many people want to avert their eyes. In its way, it's like coming by chance upon a road accident. No one wants to be seen 'gawping'.

I am so glad that it wasn't like that for me or for my mother, that the people we were joining were so accepting of how we were feeling. We stepped out of the car into arms that were held open for us. The voices we heard were voices that spoke in the kind of language we understood. We walked out of what had been a shock for us all into what I can only describe as a warm pool of consolation, and Father Tom Nicholson was there too.

Father Tom has been there for every crisis in the Barnard family. He was there when my brother died. He conducted the service for Barbara. He officiated at my father's wedding to Karin. Father Tom has been a friend and counsellor to us all at very different times in our lives. The Barnards are not the greatest communicators in the world, but we could always talk to Father Tom and when we did, he always listened.

I had to tell my brothers, my father's two sons with Barbara. The smallest brother and sister would also have to be told. I phoned Frederick and Christiaan first and then I phoned Karin. I had to tell my sister-in-law Gail so that her two children, Adam and Ashlea, could be told. My poor Pappa: his life was so full of children and grandchildren and in-laws, plus a first wife and a new ex-wife. When the time came around for family gatherings – like his last birthday party, which I organised at The Castle in Cape Town, where we all sat at one long table 'Italian style' – my father always called us 'the Full Catastrophe'.

I told you that my father was given Greek citizenship and how much he liked the healthy-living island of Crete, where he might happily have lived out his life as a fisherman or olive grower and had no use for the cardiac surgeon's skills by which he earned his living.

Nikos Kazantzakis, the author of *Zorba the Greek*, was Cretan too. Everyone remembers the film with Anthony Quinn playing Zorba, the wise and zestful Greek peasant who teaches the inhibited young Englishman, Alan Bates, about life. In one part the Bates character asks Zorba if he's married. 'Am I married?' he says. 'Am I not a man and is a man not married? Of course I'm married! A wife, a house, children, the full catastrophe.'

That was my father, and he needed no one to teach him to dance.

~

When we got back from Auntie Rita's funeral the press were waiting outside my house. Sky News were there and etv and a whole lot of people. I invited them in. I don't know quite why what happens to me at moments like this actually happens, but it does. It seems to me I can step outside myself and no matter how I feel inside, there's something even deeper inside, something like an extra surge of energy that bounces out, and I can hear myself saying: 'Yes, we have heard what happened. Yes, it is absolutely terrible news. Don't you want to come inside? I can make you tea or coffee. Why don't you come inside off the street and sit down?' I don't know why I do it. It's me, I suppose. I can't stop myself.

I always used to offer milk tart. I don't know why I did that either. I couldn't make decent milk tart if my life depended on it. I suppose it's because of the person I am. It would be funny for me to offer those little cucumber sandwiches with the crusts all cut off and anyway I couldn't waste bread with so many people going hungry and journalists would look funny eating 'shop' jam sponge cake. They always have cameras and tape recorders and such a lot of stuff with them and jam sponge crumbs get in everywhere.

I don't know what I offered them that day, but I did ask them in. I gave an interview to Sky News upstairs in my house, where we could be quiet, and downstairs Kobus watched it on television and all the while messages of condolence kept coming in from all over the world.

~

Everyone knew about the arthritis but no one seemed very focused on the asthma, even though it was something else my father lived with on a daily basis. I suppose because there's a kind of inverse glamour about a high profile pioneering surgeon whose career can be terminated by arthritis. Isn't that the kind of thing that captures people's imaginations? '*Haai, foeitog,*' they say. 'Oh, what a shame. Now that's really sad.' Isn't that why there are films about Jacqueline du Pré or such a high level of ongoing interest in Christopher Reeve? After all, wasn't he once Superman, and could fly?

Asthma is frightening. It can be fatal, as we found out, and there's nothing very glamorous about it. My father was careful always to have his asthma pump with him. We liked to go swimming together. At the townhouse complex where he lived there's a communal swimming pool. It isn't like a pool right at your front door. You have to take a little walk to get to it and you have to take your bits and pieces with you.

When we went out for a swim, I was the towel bearer. He always said: 'Have you got the towels? Have you got the front door key? Is the asthma pump there?'

It's ironic my father should die for lack of a pump. His business was with an organ he insisted was no more than a pump. He often said so, and in the beginning a few eyebrows shot up because it was considered a deeply irreverent observation to make. Of course he knew better than most people the perils of a malfunctioning 'pump' and devoted his life to the care, maintenance and repair of 'the pump'. No one needs to be told that that particular pump is a life source, but the small, innocent-looking asthma pump my father always carried with him had just as much power in it. For the lack of a pump, so very different from the one my father devoted his life to, he died.

My father had to come home from Greece. There are certain requirements that have to be met before you can bring someone home who has died in a foreign place. My father was well known and respected in Greece. He was an 'honorary Greek'. Even so, by his own wish and by the wish of us all, it was time for him to come home.

The Greek authorities were very helpful and so was the South African Ambassador to Greece, Jannie Momberg. You hear terrible stories about what can happen in a situation like this. Everywhere you turn you get caught up in bureaucracy, but I can truly say this didn't happen to me and I'm very grateful for that.

There are far easier things one has to do in this life than bring your father home in this way.

I don't know if the Barnard name helped ... and I've just read that over again and want to stop here to say something just before anyone says: 'The Barnard name? Excuse me, but just exactly how much does she think that counts for?'

My father said you should always use any tool you could to cut through red tape if it was for a good cause. My father was dead and it hurt me all over. If calling myself Cleopatra Queen of the Nile would have helped me bring him home again, I would have called myself that too.

I was in my house in Higgovale with people coming and going and bringing things to eat for 'in case' and saying how sorry they were. It was like Waterloo station downstairs with all that was going on, and somewhere in between there were cooking smells because someone was making something to eat. There I was on the phone with my list of numbers right next to me, phoning every-one I could think of who might help and dropping the names of just about everyone I knew as well as the names of one or two people I didn't really know at all. I was willing to do whatever it took.

While we were planning the funeral, while we were phoning Athens, Crete, this one and the next one, my nerves were finished. On top of everything else, including my worry about long distance phone bills and how they can bankrupt you, my husband Kobus – whom I love dearly – keeps talking in the way you're supposed to talk about dead people. You know what I mean, that way that is all very calm and quiet and polite. He keeps talking about 'bringing back the remains' the way well-brought-up people are meant to. It just comes out. He can't help it. But I don't want to know about 'remains'. I just want my father to come home.

I know there are things that have to be done. There's a cremation to arrange. My father wants his ashes to be taken to the town where he was born, Beaufort West in the Great Karoo. My youngest little brother, Karin's son Armin, is horrified by the idea of cremation. Karin phones and asks me to speak to him. The poor child is beyond consolation. He keeps weeping in the most pitiful way and saying he doesn't want Dadda to be burned. He doesn't want Dadda to be burned. I start crying too and against my father's wishes and despite having to change all the arrangements I give Armin my word this won't happen.

I promise him and he trusts me and I would never break my word to him. He knows that and it makes him feel better.

I remembered then about the time my brother died. It was such a terrible time for us all. His children were very young and it was decided that they ought not to attend his funeral. For some or other reason they were packed off to a picnic on a farm somewhere. It was a decision made in the best possible faith, to spare making a painful experience even more painful for them, but subsequently his son, Adam, minded very much.

Gail told me how he'd cried bitterly and said over and over

again: 'Mommy, why didn't you let me say goodbye to Daddy?' It was absolutely heart-rending. I could hardly bear to hear it.

Many people say the saddest thing in the world is for a parent to lose a child. My mother and my father, when he was alive, could most surely have answered to that, but losing a parent, especially for a very young child, is also a most terrible rift.

I had learnt from what happened when my brother died, although I stood outside then in a way I did not with my father. When my brother died he had been a part of his own smaller family unit within the larger family. He had his wife Gail and his two children and they were, as they should be, far higher up the priority list than a sister can ever be.

With my father it was different. At the end of his life I spent a lot of time with my father. I felt very close to him. I wanted a chance to do more for him. I felt the wrench of his going impact on my own life with a very great force, and it was different.

Armin had a right to say goodbye. None of us would have denied him that or willingly have let him go through life with that terrible mental image of his Dadda 'being burned'.

I myself haven't had time to think about these final technicalities. All I want is for my father to be brought home in the proper way. I just want him home, that's all. I think about his Greek citizenship and the generosity of the Greeks in giving him such a great gift.

I think how he loved Greece, not just the place or the fact that the Cretans are so healthy that they could have put him right out of business. It was more than that that he loved. He loved the ethos and he loved the people and it occurs to me that you can love a country other than the place where you were born. You can love any country in the world you care to and feel a sense of kinship with it, but when the time comes your soul pulls you home. It's a blood call and I can't imagine anyone who can resist it.

My father wanted, it was his express wish in the end, to come home, to complete the circle of his life and lie at the end in the place where his life began.

Do you know the Great Karoo? My father likened it to the State of Arizona in the USA, and it is great indeed. It's a vast, seemingly empty scrubland where the sun reflects up off the ground and puts a shimmer on everything in summer and the winters are so achingly cold the water in the outside troughs freezes over. It's sheep country, mainly, and my father had two farms there called Ratelfontein and Bloemhof and he stocked them with game.

My father loved these farms in the heartland and he loved hunting. In his young days, when my mother first knew him and took him home to Okahandja to meet her parents, he went hunting there too. Sometimes I think that perhaps it wasn't just my mother's wonderful eyes and her other undoubted attractions that drew him to her. I think the farm clinched it. My father was in love with my mother but he was in love with the wilderness too.

In his later life he and his sons and Adam, my late brother's son, enjoyed nothing more than going out hunting in the back of a bakkie at night. These are the men in our family and these expeditions brought them even closer together, and I think he liked that.

In the Great Karoo the sky is immense. The air is thin and clear and people come and go from the landscape and live on in the stories that those who come after tell about them, or in the few words engraved on the headstones in the little churchyards outside the towns. That's how their passing is noted, while the land just goes on. It's right that my father should have returned.

I think about the Father Brown stories and the 'twitch upon the string'. You know, that story about the man who had a string tied to his ankle, but the string was long enough to let him go as far around the world as he liked. Yet, when the moment came, the string was still attached to his ankle and the gentlest pull would be more than enough to let him know it was time to return.

So it was with my father.

I had been to Cape Town's airport to see him off safely. I would be there to see him come home and Kobus would be with me. Frederick and Christiaan came. So did Karin and Armin, and Father Tom and Dene were there too. We were allowed to wait for him in the VIP lounge and Kobus and I were there first, but the others had said they were coming and I knew they'd be there. There were some things that struck me. A funeral parlour, AVBOB, telephoned to ask if they might have the privilege of handling all the arrangements free of charge. They wanted to do that as a gift for my father and we were grateful and very much touched by this.

I didn't want a black car. I hated the idea of it. There were never any dark things about my father. He was a lover of laughter and energy and light. I had said nothing about the car. And I forgot they'd been so kind that I didn't want to start giving orders or making demands. It was to be their tribute and I knew they wanted to do it their way, but they sent a white car without my ever having to ask them.

The Greeks were kind too. My father came home in a plain wooden coffin. He would have liked that. Despite all the reams that were written about him, my father saw himself as a plain man and a simple wooden coffin would have suited him just fine.

My father always liked coming home. No matter where he'd been in the world or how exciting his adventures, coming home was the best part of all. He'd said so. I would have liked him to see it, to see for himself this last homecoming.

When my father came home to his own country, this strange mixed-up country that he loved perhaps even more than he realised, all of us were there waiting to meet him. Frederick,

Christiaan, Karin, Armin, Kobus and me, all of the Barnards, neat, tidy, present and accounted for. The Full Catastrophe waiting to tell their Pappa, Dad, Dadda that he was back with us, back where he belonged and that we were there just where we'd always be, right there waiting for him when he needed us.

14

Coming home

*'I would like a Karoo stone brought in from the veld
where I walked as a boy. I want it placed in the garden
of the house in Beaufort West where I grew up. On it
I would like a plaque saying, "I've come home again."'*

My father was quite specific about his final wishes. He stated them
on national television on *People of the South* when he gave his last
interview in South Africa, shortly before he died.

That too was my father's way. When he and Barbara parted, he
addressed a letter to her in a national Sunday paper asking her to
come back to him. He was not what you call particularly 'private'.
He was definitely not a person who bottled things up. If you were
looking for someone you could rely on to blurt out exactly what
was on his mind, then he was your man.

I think it must be a bit odd to ask someone, especially someone
no longer young, what they want to happen to them when they
die. Once you agree to go on a show, though, you know the journalist can ask you anything and so I don't suppose my father
minded too much.

It was a fair enough question and he gave a plain answer: the
answer at the head of this chapter. Of course we as a family
intended to honour his wishes.

AVBOB, who came in the white car to the airport, drove my father's ashes to Beaufort West. (Because in the end he *was* cremated, but I shall tell you about that in a little while.) My friend Caro Wiese, who is kind, practical and generous, came over at once to see what she could do to make things easy for us. She hired a plane so that I could fly to Beaufort West for the memorial service and my mother came with me. So did Susan Vosloo, the wonderful paediatric heart surgeon who had performed operations on some of the children whose treatment was sponsored by the Christiaan Barnard Foundation, and her husband, anaesthetist Anton Ferreira. They had obligations that would have made the 450 km journey by car very difficult for them. We also made space for Father Tom and for Dene on board the plane and Tiaan sat on the toilet seat at the back.

The telephone seemed never to stop ringing. People were unendingly kind and generous. It was a terrible time, but I felt that our family was on the receiving end of a great outpouring of love and sympathy. I think they wanted to show that at the end of it all, my father, with all his powers and with all his frailties, had been a major public figure in this country. I think people wanted us to know they acknowledged this and respected him for it.

My father had been so full of contradictions. I liked it when the journalist Bob Molloy, who covered the first heart transplant, wrote this story about him:

> The story was a winner. Small girl dying of heart failure. Home town collects cash to send her halfway across the planet to be operated on by the world's most famous heart surgeon. Mother too ill to accompany her but grandmother steps in as nurse companion.
>
> The scene-setters practically wrote themselves. Brave grandmother carries dying child in arms down steps of aircraft. Pictures of purple-lipped girl, breathless, pale, and

beautiful – doomed unless the famous surgeon can perform a miracle. Background stories on the family – sick mother, anguished father, tense siblings. Tests. More tests. Hope. Hope fading. Barnard won't talk to the press but grandmother gives me an exclusive.

The child had a congenital heart condition. Discovered at birth. Surgical treatment refused by her own country's doctors. Child too ill, take her home to die, they said. Family despair. See Barnard on television doing his 'heart as a pump' routine. Friend urges them to write. Fearful letter querying cost of operation and child's chances. Warm, personal reply (from the world's busiest surgeon?) and an undertaking to carry out 'any required surgery, free of charge'.

The story was a crowd-puller, a smiling weepie that stayed on the front pages for days. There were more angles than I had time to write. Tests showed the child had major heart defects. The chances of a successful surgical intervention looked bleak. But, Barnard tells the grandmother, he would operate if the family had the courage to accept the outcome.

Privately, I wondered why a successful surgeon with the world at his feet should accept patients who had been turned down elsewhere by equally competent surgeons. Surgeons perhaps who didn't want their record spoiled by no-hopers?

It was a facet of Barnard of which I was to see more – a man who quite frankly didn't give a damn for conventions, whether medical, social or political. A doctor who cared for his patients with an almost naïve honesty. So naïve in fact that at one press conference he insisted he had 'killed' a patient through inept surgery. He demanded, and got, high standards from his heart team – anything less than perfection he'd regarded as inept.

On the occasion the hospital's public relations machine moved fast to explain that what the professor really meant was ... The explanation was hardly helped by Barnard's over-the-shoulder one-liner to the press – 'They're talking crap.'

Came the day of the operation. In newspaper parlance we had a running story, a cliffhanger with a dying heroine and a good guy who wanted to save her. Would she make it? Could he do it? From reader reaction, we could have sold as many hankies as we did newspapers.

The grandmother gratefully accepted my offer to drive her to the hospital and sit with her throughout the ordeal, unaware she was my passport to the action.

That's how, hours later, stiff with boredom, I was the only reporter who saw Prof. Chris Barnard burst into the waiting room, mask around his neck and still gowned from the operating theatre. Grinning from ear to ear, he grabbed the grandmother in a bear hug, whirled the startled woman around the floor in an impromptu waltz and yelled, 'She's fine, she's okay, she's going to be all right.'

This was a different Barnard. This was Barnard, the winner, the one who laughed and loved the world. Barnard the softie. Barnard of the big heart and warm smile.

Bob Molloy had seen the part of my father that was 'the cheeky kid who loved giving the finger to authority'. It didn't do my dad much good.

Because of his growing profile around the world, children flooded in from everywhere seeking treatment at Groote Schuur. They came from Africa. They came from Europe, where they had very many good doctors and excellent facilities of their own. They came from behind the Iron Curtain, where very probably, in those days, they did not. They were all colours and all creeds and they were all given treatment in the same way as our own state patients were. They paid according to their means. If they couldn't pay, then their treatment was free. My father would not have worked any other way.

There was a story my uncle Marius told my father and he never forgot it. It must have touched something deep inside him.

An African boy of about ten was brought into hospital with severe cardiac failure brought on by rheumatic fever. An operation had to be performed on him and it was a very difficult thing to do because his state of health was already so precarious. No one likes to lose a patient, my father least of all, but it soon became clear that the boy was dying. My uncle told my father that he'd visited the child, who was in an oxygen tent, and asked him whether there was anything he wanted, and what he asked for was a piece of bread.

My father could hardly bear to tell this story, it moved him so much. A sufficient diet, more bread, earlier in his life might have meant life itself to this child. By the time he was admitted to hospital there were not skills enough in this world that could save him and if there was one thing my father hated, it was powerlessness.

He was filled with pity for the suffering of humankind. He found unbearable all those things in life beyond individual control which render a human being powerless: racial discrimination, lack of material resources, even the condition of simply being still a child, which when you consider it is the most powerless state of all.

It was against government policy, but my father refused to segregate his wards. Now that his profile was so public, he could do that and hospital bureaucracy could do very little about it. It was because of him that a South African hospital was the focus of so much world attention. They had a wonderful one-man PR team in my father. He certainly spread the name of Groote Schuur Hospital far and wide and brought in a considerable amount of much-needed funding.

Nothing's for nothing, though. Desegregating certain wards would seem a small enough price to pay. You would have thought they would have understood that you can't have things your own way all the time, but I'm not all that sure they did.

At this stage, as he was beginning to feel the power of his popularity and public image, he began to inject a strong anti-apartheid line into his public statements. This didn't make him very popular.

Many VIP privileges that were given when the powers-that-be were claiming him as their own were taken away. Small things, like the use of private lounges at airports and being fast-tracked through the formalities, were withdrawn. 'Orders,' the airport officials always told him, slightly embarrassed. He didn't mind. He just went ahead with his life in his own way.

My father had a sense of irony and a sense of humour as well, as the following story shows. On one of his lecture tours of America he had a day to spare between speaking engagements and the United States Air Force put a plane at his disposal to take him anywhere he liked. He asked to go to Houston to see some of the work his colleague Dr Denton Cooley was busy with.

When he arrived at Houston there was a crowd waiting to greet him, a red carpet laid down on the runway and a military band thumping out music at full blast. Dr Cooley was waiting for him in the airport building.

'As he stepped forward to meet me,' my father wrote, 'he greeted me with an outstretched hand and a twinkle in his eye. He said, disarmingly, "Hi, boy! What's your name?"'

My father had said afterwards that if there was any risk of the splendour of his arrival going to his head or giving him any undue sense of self-importance, there was no possibility of it after that greeting. He never forgot that incident.

⁓

This was the man we had come to this small town in the middle of nowhere to bury. I thought back on his glory days, which I had watched from the sidelines like everyone else, and it seemed to me, looking back, that those days had had a magical quality about them. There was a light and it seemed to shine around them and it shone so brightly it could make you sad.

When we reached the town television crews were already there setting up gantries for their equipment.

The memorial service was to be held in the Old Dutch Reformed Mission Church where my father had pumped the bellows for the organ in the old days when his father was preacher there and his mother played the organ.

In those days the churches were kept separate. The coloured people of the town attended my grandfather's church. The more affluent white community, more than likely dressed up to the nines, had a church of their own, but there are some seductions too potent to ignore. On their way home, after their own service was over, you'd often find white churchgoers making a detour past the old Mission Church. It wasn't that one dose of the Lord's word just wasn't enough for them. What they wanted was to hear the coloured congregation raising their wonderful voices in praise and thanks to the Lord for the mercies he had seen fit to heap upon them.

My father always said he'd turned his back on the Dutch Reformed Church because it stood idly by while his father's coloured congregation were turned out of their church and moved to the outskirts of the town while their church was converted into a sports hall.

He said he would have nothing to do with 'men of God' who turned a blind eye when the Nationalist government disobeyed the second most important of the Ten Commandments, which was to 'Love thy neighbour as thyself.'

It offended everything in him that men who wore the cloth as his own father once had did nothing to stop apartheid, but instead kept their heads averted while they combed the Bible to find suitable passages to make a dreadful wrong look like God's will.

All the same, things had changed and he was back and the town was out *en fête* to welcome him. I think Frederick and Christiaan, who value a private life above just about anything else, found it rather off-putting.

It wasn't funereal at all. In fact it had a bit of a party atmosphere about it. A local guesthouse had put accommodation at our disposal. That night, the night before the service, we did have a party, right there in the middle of the Karoo where it was still cold at night and there are so many stars you can hardly bear to look up at them.

My father would have loved it. I just wish he could have seen it.

Everyone was welcome. People in the town kept coming over and asking if the funeral was 'private'. I kept saying, 'Of course not, everybody's welcome.' In the end I think 'everyone' came. The church was full and there were chairs in the street. It's like that in the small towns. People like a good funeral. They like to say their goodbyes.

My father had been cremated in Cape Town before we went to Beaufort West. In the end, having been taken to see his Dadda and say his goodbyes, Armin came to terms with it and agreed.

I was the one who in the end became uncertain. Everyone tells you such funny stories about cremation and how you can never be certain it's your own person's ashes the crematorium gives back to you. I know it's ridiculous, but I wanted to be absolutely sure. I told the man at the crematorium this. I said I would stay there while the cremation took place but I wanted him to give me his word that when I left that place it was my own father's ashes I took with me and nobody else's. He promised me it would be.

When the time came to lay him finally to rest, the ashes were handed to me in two beautiful little boxes with engraved plates on them. I was happy with that. They seemed simple and more appropriate, somehow, than the very ornate coffin the ashes had made the last leg of the journey in from Cape Town to Beaufort West. Perhaps this was because one represented the public man and the other his inner self – or perhaps I'm just being fanciful.

My brother's son Adam was very nice to Armin at the funeral.

Armin is very young still. Adam spoke to him about fishing. I suppose that's the kind of thing men understand. Adam had lost his own father and I suppose he would be the best one to know what to say.

Armin, being the youngest, carried one of the boxes and Christiaan, the one named for my father, carried the other.

I'd asked Karin about the flowers. Flower Walker, the famous Cape Town florist with the most appropriate name in the business, had said how much she would like to be responsible for the flowers. What would we like? Karin had the last word and her choice was exactly right. She said my father would have liked flowers from the veld. Veld flowers are always simple and beautiful and bloom for a very short time, whenever the spring rains fall, and in every single way they were appropriate.

It was Christiaan who thought of the roses. There is a rose named for my father and there was a display of these roses in a big bowl at the entrance of the church so that each churchgoer could take one and put it in a vase in front of the pulpit.

Each of the family carried one of these roses and placed them on the boxes carrying his ashes when they were laid to rest in the garden. Lara, the littlest one, the one who had had least of her Dadda, had her rose too and no one was forgotten.

I was sorry my daughter Karen couldn't be there but my father died on 1 September and at the time of the service, 11 September had just happened. Karen, in New York at the time, got stuck there and couldn't get a flight home.

My niece Ashlea was there, though. She's a lovely girl and very special to me. She looks very much like her father, my late brother.

Every time I looked at her I had a feeling that in some way she carried him inside her. I was so conscious of that presence. It gave me warmth and strength and I told her so afterwards.

When it was all over it was strange. It was strange leaving him there. I knew once the plane had taken off, once people had packed up their cars and turned toward Cape Town, Beaufort West would be quiet again. It would be timeless, a small dream-town in the heartland of Africa.

I thought then I would write a book called *Hoe om jou Pa lekker te begrawe (How to Give Your Dad a Really Good Send-off)*. I have a friend, Myrtle, who lost her father just before my Dad died, and we agreed that it's important for oneself to have done the right thing. It rounds things off properly.

I knew it was right. I knew it was time. I knew that the wheel of his life had come full circle and I wondered then, as I wonder now, how much of him it was that we actually left there and how much we continue to carry with us.

15

Children who have changed my life

'Think big and your deeds will grow,
Think small and you'll fall behind,
Think that you can and you will.
It's all in the state of mind.' [Anon]

Having spoken about death, I think it's a good thing to switch straight back into life again. Every old platitude you ever heard becomes irritating only because it's true and so I am going to say it: life goes on and life, inevitably, is about the next generation.

Anyone who knows me knows that one way or another there have been a great many children in my life. I have been a child myself. I have two children. Goodness knows, our family is pretty liberally peppered with children. After an abortive try at social work in my first year at Stellenbosch I went on to do a teaching diploma. It was called HPOD and we called it *Hard Probeer om te Dop*, which means 'try hard to fail'. Before I qualified as a teacher I had been a nanny. After I qualified I went on to become remedial teacher. So it's not too difficult to see where my heart lies.

You don't need a reason to love children. You love them because they're there and because they accept you just as you are. It doesn't matter what size you are, or what colour or even what language you speak. Children are always prepared to give you the benefit of the doubt. I have had times in my life when I have had reason to be grateful for that.

Once when my father was asked what, in his opinion, his greatest achievement was, he said it was a difficult technical procedure he'd mastered that enabled children born with damaged hearts to have the defects surgically corrected.

He said he found it difficult to understand how God could allow a child to be born abnormal. The aim of the foundation named for him is of course to address exactly this problem and to help as many children as funds allow.

One of my father's last great joys was going to Cape Town's airport to welcome a Russian boy who had been sponsored by the Foundation to come to South Africa for life-changing heart surgery.

One of his last great satisfactions was that the operation was successful and that the boy left here to go forward with nothing physically to prevent him from having a full and happy life.

My own first 'children' got me by default, and it all had to do with the fat thing. On the *Oriana* when I was Mej. Viets and had won all the prizes, I began eating again and it was a problem. If you think being Mej. Viets was all beer and skittles, I can tell you that it wasn't.

Now I wasn't just fat, I was fat with a problem and the problem was that I was no longer responsible only to myself. I'd taken Annetjie Theron's Wonderslim, I'd taken the cruise and I'd taken all the other prizes *Rapport* and all the other sponsors were offering, which meant I had contractual obligations to them.

Getting thin was one thing. The rest of the story was that I had to stay that way, and that was another thing altogether and it wasn't so easy. The more I realised this, the more guilty I began to feel. (You know, when you come to think about it, Calvinism has really a lot to answer for in this life.) There was a film test lined up for me. I kept being tactfully reminded of it. The more I thought about that, the guiltier I felt. I kept remembering that a movie camera is supposed to automatically put seven pounds onto a person's weight and how all the famous film stars, when you see them in real life, are actually tiny, little itty-bitty people.

I knew it was true. Dean Martin, who was an admirer of my father, had once invited me to come and visit him and stay in his house. I met Raquel Welch there and she was small, much smaller than she looked on the screen. Frank Sinatra visited too and they all watched movies together and thinking back on that occasion, it occurred to me that they were all small.

I began to believe that that visit had been like a visit to Lilliput, that I had been the only person of even vaguely normal size there. Dean Martin had given me a signed photograph of himself; I have it still. (Famous people often like to do that. They do it without your even asking them. Don't ask me why, but they do.) He wrote on it what a nice girl I was. Nowhere did he say what a thin girl I was.

When I thought about that, I ate even more, and there was another problem too. I had to be weighed just as a precaution, to see that when I got to Los Angeles, prior to having my film test and making it big in the movie business, I would still be in mint condition.

I don't know if anyone remembers this, but before Roseanne Barr, Hollywood didn't have too much time for fat ladies.

You remember I told you that I could tell you how to get the optimum reading out of any scale ever invented, on a massive cruise liner in a mid-Atlantic swell? This is how I discovered this, and I am eternally grateful for those swells. I stood there waiting for them, just like the surfers do when they're in surfing competitions, and when I felt an advantageous one coming up, I quickly jumped on the scale.

I couldn't get away with it. I knew that. At best it could only be a temporary measure. It was soon very obvious to Annetjie, who was chaperoning me on the cruise, and to me that there could be no brilliant movie career for me. We both accepted that, and there was something else too. Anneke was missing her husband and wanted to get home. She'd made up her mind that when we got to Los Angeles we'd fly back to New York and then, courtesy of *Rapport* and our sponsors, we'd fly back to South Africa.

That was fine for her. She had a husband who just couldn't wait to see her again. Besides which, she was thin, but it wasn't so fine for me. I'd signed a contract. If I went back fat I'd have to give back all my prizes.

I had to make a quick plan. What I decided was not to go home, but to jump ship. If I could, I would have stayed on that cruise ship forever and never touched land, but my predicament brought me face to face with reality. That wasn't going to happen. What I needed was a job, and pretty damn quickly.

I approached a woman I'd seen who was travelling with two little boys, Joshua and Benjamin. 'Excuse me,' I said. 'Do you need a nanny?' I don't know what she must have thought, but now that I'm older and have raised and travelled with two children myself I can imagine. I can also imagine how my mother must have felt, travelling with my brother Andre and me, not quite a year apart in age, on a cargo boat from South Africa to New York all those years before, and then flying to Minneapolis to join my father.

She looked at me as if I'd been delivered from heaven and hired me there and then. When we got to Southampton there was a big Daimler waiting to collect us and I was ushered into the car with the rest of the family. There I sat, the nanny with a baby in her arms, having put behind any hope I might once have had of seeing my name up in lights (I had never really believed it would be, anyway) and having made a career change in mid-ocean.

My employers were Mr and Mrs Ball and lived in Prince's Gate, which is quite a name-drop address if you're in that frame of mind. Mr Ball worked for the advertising agency Ogilvy & Mather. His wife was Australian and had once been a model. She was on a good eating programme and I thought that might help me. I used to be sent to Harrods to buy New Zealand lamb (I suppose she must have had quite a lot of New Zealand lamb when she was growing up in Australia). I could have every good, healthy thing that I liked to eat, and I did, but even so I filled up on Purity baby food. Can you believe that? You do that when you're fat. You know that story: 'Spoonful for you, spoonful for me. Here comes the little red engine right into your mouth. Spoonful for you, spoonful for me.'

That was me in Prince's Gate, but I was happy there. Prince's Gate is very near Hyde Park and I loved being a Hyde Park nanny and pushing one of those big, high-wheeled prams around. I didn't think of it then, but I think of it now, that I could have put on my CV 'Hyde Park Nanny'. I'm sure that in certain quarters that counts for quite a lot in the job market.

The Balls became a kind of surrogate family to me and they were immensely kind. They had a lady who cleaned their house called Mrs Hall and so I learnt there not to get your consonants mixed up and to pronounce my vowels carefully, which probably helped my South African accent along a little bit.

Lady Churchill was a neighbour of the Balls and the doorman (I told you it was a good neighbourhood) told me one day she'd like to meet me. She lived in a beautifully furnished apartment and was very nice to me. She was what I suppose the English would call gracious and we had a pleasant conversation. She had the most beautiful English accent: I was absolutely fascinated by it and could have listened to her for hours. I was invited to visit her again whenever I liked, and I did sometimes go to see her.

My mother came to visit me while I was in London. She was quite wonderful. Only a mother, and most particularly my mother, would come to London as a part of a trip to Europe –

which was not an everyday thing for her as it was for my father – and help me with the ironing that was part of my job.

She was travelling with a friend and they stayed in an apartment in the same building. She asked me if I wouldn't join them and see something of Europe with them. They were keen that I should do so, but I didn't want to go. I was going through that phase where you tend to want to stay in your own space.

First my space was the *Oriana*, where I considered myself one of the family and spent so much time hanging around with the crew that they would call me a ship's fixture, and I must say I rather liked it.

My space now was with the Ball family, where I was just another nanny strolling Hyde Park, unconditionally loved by the charges into whose care they'd been placed. I liked those secure confines, where I knew the parameters and nothing more was demanded of me than that I just be myself. I didn't feel ready for the wider world yet, not even for a holiday with my mother, but I knew one day I would have to make the break. I should have been braver.

I also saw my father during that year in London. He and Barbara were in Italy. They were staying with the Mondadoris, Giorgio and his wife Nara, members of the famous publishing family which had published his first book. He asked me if I wouldn't come to spend some time with them there.

The house, when I eventually reached it, wasn't a house at all. It was more like a palace surrounded by gardens with cherry trees, immaculate lawns and a swimming pool.

It was a good time but it wasn't the best time, if you know what I mean. Time had passed and events not shared had created a gap between my father and me. To correct that we would have needed time to fill in all those unshared spaces. I knew this wouldn't happen. I had long since realised that this kind of time, quality time, if you like to call it that, was something that would not be so easy to come by for my father and me in these new days.

The Mondadori house was pretty much how you would expect such a house to be. You walked into it and it kind of swallowed you up. Barbara was used to such places and comfortable in them, but I wasn't.

Also, it's a bit of a culture shock to be a Hyde Park nanny one day and the next day to find yourself moving in high society, where people are thin and sophisticated and beautifully dressed all the time.

There was something else too. Barbara was pregnant, very beautifully pregnant with Frederick, at that time. She was very kind to me, as she always was. I had my usual problem with fat and with clothes. She said if I liked I could help myself to some of her maternity clothes and then at least I could billow around in style.

Let me tell you here, it is a very sobering thing when someone's nine-months-pregnant clothes are too small for you. It can take you one of two ways – straight back to Wonderslim or to the fridge – and I took the coward's way. I befriended the Mondadori staff as I had the crew on the *Oriana* and the staff at Groote Schuur when I was there on my weight reduction programme.

I was back to my old tricks. Once you know the staff, easy access to the fridge is a cinch. I didn't take much. It isn't as if anyone could have opened the fridge after I'd been there and seen tooth marks on the Parma ham, or a big bite out of the salmon. I suppose I could have had anything, but I only ate yoghurt; but even so, the fact that it was only yoghurt and not something more extravagant didn't make it better. In its own way the smallness of it only made everything worse.

Even so, life isn't only the story of one little failure piling up hard against another. Leon Norgarb, the tennis coach, was there with his wife Sue. He said I was *simpatico* and I suppose that has to count for something, and when I got back to London there was something else too.

On the *Oriana* I had met a wonderful officer. His name was Alan Trotter and he came from Torquay. We sort of fell in love and he seemed to adore me and I was so grateful for that. I in my turn thought he was marvellous: I could talk as much as I liked and he'd just sit there and listen. I didn't know it then but I know it now. Silence is a great aphrodisiac. Have you ever sat opposite a nice-looking man who just looks into your eyes and says nothing while you babble on?

You can't help thinking what a nice man he is. He is actually listening to me, you think. That shows he's not only nice but intelligent as well and you go on talking and he goes on looking and the next thing you know, without him even having to say one single word, it's a romance.

When I was in Prince's Gate Alan was at home in Torquay. He used to telephone me. 'Can't I come and visit you?' he'd say. 'I love you so much. Let me come and visit you.'

'No,' I'd shriek. 'Not this week. Come next week.'

And so it went on.

The trouble is that on the ship I'd been thinner. I thought if I could only put him off I'd lose about 50 pounds in a week and if he came the next week that would be fine – and so, of course, it went on and on.

In the end he said he didn't care. 'I can't wait any longer,' he said. 'I have to see you. I'm coming to London.'

What could I do? I said he could come and we arranged to meet at one of the big railway stations, and I was desperate. I'd got fatter and fatter. Not even the jeans with the safety pins to give just a little bit more space to fit into them worked any more. All I could get into were Laura Ashley dresses. You remember those dresses? Like little bell tents all covered with flowers. That's all I could wear and it's what I went to the station in to meet this man who loved me so much.

He came just as he said he would. I was waiting for him just as

I said I'd be. I suppose in its way it was like a scene from *High Noon* (only without the guns and the grudge) and it wasn't a case of 'the closer he gets, the better you look'. It was a case of the closer he got, the more obvious it became that I'd put on so much weight that he didn't recognise me at all. He walked right past me and then did a double take, but he was a nice man. He wasn't the man I eventually married, but he was a man who could look into a girl's eyes and when he eventually got a chance to say something, what he said with absolute truth shining in his face was: 'I don't care if you've put on weight. What difference can that make to me? It's you that I love and I love you just the same.'

You show me a girl with a weight problem who hasn't dreamed of meeting a man like that. In fact, if you can show me a middle-aged woman, who even after many years of happily married life wouldn't still have a soft spot for a man who could love you like that, I would be very surprised.

There were other things I was thinking about too as I wheeled my little charges around Hyde Park. I didn't mind being a nanny. Nannies were nothing new to me. But my fellow nannies in Hyde Park were not like the African nannies I'd known at home, the ones who had raised so many white children of my generation and formed our early years. As I strolled Hyde Park, with no children of my own yet, enjoying Jonathan and Benjamin and the other children out taking the air, I was struck by how different Hyde Park was from the places I grew up in and the places of my heart. I suppose I felt a little bit homesick. It was all such a long way away and I missed it. At the same time I was having an opportunity to read the newspapers and watch television in a different country, and it gave me time to think.

I thought what an irony it was that while those black women in my home country were raising white women's children, the raising of their own children was being left to others. Many justify this similarity by saying that the black nannies need the money to support their families, but this doesn't make it right. Children need to be with their parents. So much of what they become in later life stems from where they start off. In my adult life I have worked at poor schools and I've worked at more affluent schools and one thing I've learnt is that there is no amount of time or money in the world that can compensate for the love and care of a parent.

My father, who some people had called the 'darling' of the then (Nationalist) government, had indicated this same irony, but he'd put it in a different way. Having been asked to speak to the Afrikaans Chamber of Commerce (and the fact that Afrikaners had their own Chamber of Commerce tells you something about how things were at that time), he was introduced as 'one of the greatest Afrikaners South Africa has ever produced' and there was loud applause and lots of cheering.

Did it not occur to them, he asked, how strange it was that children who were lovingly raised by black women, and other women of colour, could not be cared for by them if they happened to find themselves in hospital?

This sounds very strange, thinking back on it now. It looks very funny written down in the paragraph above. It's hard to believe that in those days white patients were tended only by white nursing staff, yet that was the case.

My father went on to say that whenever he went abroad there were a great many questions fired at him and he was now wondering whether these great movers and shakers in his own country, at present seated before him, had any answers for him.

He asked if they had ever asked themselves why white children played with black and coloured friends in their little towns, yet when they grew up were not allowed to compete with each other on the sportsfield.

It did not go down well. For a while there was absolute silence.

Then someone from the back offered an answer and it was a typical answer of that time.

'If that's the kind of question you get asked when you're out of the country, then you can tell them we do these things because it's our business, not theirs. If you think it's so wrong, you can go and join them if you like.'

The president of the Chamber decided question time was over and the evening was at an end, but there was more to it than simply the end of those particular proceedings.

It was the first time my father had spoken out against apartheid in public. Things would not be easy for him from now on. There were people he knew who would have to decide whether or not it was politic to be seen with him.

It was the kind of thing that didn't worry him at all, but he was hissed and booed, which I think might have been a first for him. I think that by that stage he'd got rather used to being liked!

In Heidelberg in Germany, he'd addressed a group of students who, he'd been warned, were politically fiery and anti-South African. He started that address by sailing straight in and asking them if they knew a certain student drinking song he knew was popular at that university.

Of course they did. He started singing it. I suppose that must have caught them a bit off guard. My father was a great many things, but musical wasn't one of them. Our friend Father Tom Nicholson had heard him play the ukulele and said it made you think of a tom cat out for a night on the tiles, having such a good time and having it so loudly, that you wanted to go out and throw a bucket of water over him. In any case, it seemed to break the ice in Heidelberg. Not that the students didn't have questions. They did, and my father did his best to answer them.

As usual, he couldn't please everyone. A faculty member told the press rather icily that 'drunken singsongs are hardly the image expected of a professor of medicine'. But of course, *he* hadn't been the one facing the barrage of unanswerable questions.

The whole world had questions in those days, none of them easy to answer, and because of his travels and his high profile my father often found himself in the firing line.

Even so, with all its problems, I missed my home. Perhaps it was because of its problems that I missed it. I wanted to come back, but there was that guilt thing again. Then one day, while I was still in London, *Rapport* phoned up looking for me. Someone on the other end of the line asked if 'Deirdre Barnard, Mej. Viets', could be found at that number.

'No,' I said. 'I'm sorry. She doesn't live here any more.'

It wasn't true, but in a way it was. My time with the Balls had come to an end, not so much as a physical time but as a space in my life. I'd always known that it was going to be a part of my life, not all of it. I couldn't go on hiding forever, not on a cruise liner, not in an apartment in Prince's Gate, not anonymously, just another nanny among the all the other nannies in Hyde Park, and certainly not inside a nice comforting coating of lard. The time had come to go home.

I was still worrying about letting *Rapport* down, so I came home incognito. My mother was living in Pretoria then and I phoned her from Johannesburg's airport. I was back. I had to get my life into some kind of order.

I was still a subject short on my primary teacher's diploma. For the moment, however, teaching was out for me and my mother got me a job working in a porcelain factory, where I packed crockery. I began to feel more grounded. I must say that my mother has always provided a secure, safe haven for me and for my brother. If we were with our mother, we knew we were safe. I packed porcelain, I lost weight and when I was ready for change again, I came to Cape Town.

My father then got me a job with Sol Kerzner, the Sun King. I was assigned to the Edward Hotel in Durban and then to the Elangeni, and a wonderful young woman called Suzy Coleman trained me as a PRO. Then I was sent to Mauritius to be in charge of all the sporting activities at the hotel there and my father and Barbara came to see me, to see how I was getting along.

The answer to which was that in one way I was getting along fine. Who could not be fine on an Indian Ocean holiday island like Mauritius, with everyone just about as relaxed as they're ever going to be and out for nothing but a good time? If there were only someone who had known how to cut loose the moorings I suppose in its way it wouldn't have been all that different from my days on the *Oriana*. Only this time I was one of the crew, just like I always wanted to be, and who could ask for anything more?

The truth is that things were different. I'd changed. I felt like a ghost. There I was among beautiful, nice people – yet I had found myself in a world not really ever intended for me. The people in that world were as kind and welcoming as people could be, but I wasn't really one of them and I knew I never would be.

The time had come to grow up. I had a whole life still ahead of me and I wanted to do something with it that could be considered worthwhile. I decided to go back to Stellenbosch, to university, to finish my primary teacher's diploma. In this way I took my first step into what I came to consider my calling, which was working with children as a teacher.

A word here about working with children and my previous time at university. I know my father was not universally beloved in his life, but when I was a young student it didn't help to have a lecturer who kept snarling at me: 'And you? Who do you think you are? You think your father is so famous.'

I don't know how you are supposed to respond to something like this, but you can look at a face like that and see just by the facial expression that this person is not really going to be interested in your story that goes halfway round the block about how much you wish you could go back and have your father be un-famous again.

You just sit there and keep yourself inside yourself the best way you can and a long time afterwards you realise you've learnt something. It isn't fair to lay a parent's successes or failures at the door of a child – not on any child – and if you elect to be a teacher, which is a very great privilege, or to work with children, you should learn also to leave your own 'baggage' out of it. Someone truly born to teach would never do something like this.

~

My first teaching job was as 'governess' for an artist in Hout Bay near Cape Town. She had a dyslexic son and she'd elected to have him tutored privately because of his particular needs. He was my first 'problem' child and being for a short time a part of his life. Seeing how warmly his mother interacted with him, and what results could be achieved with focus and patience and love, was my first view of the road that would lead me to remedial teaching.

My time with that family was also my introduction to an alternative view of life. When I say that we sat among the daisies and meditated, I don't mean it to sound dismissive. There is a lot to be said for daisies and meditation and quiet.

I don't know if you have noticed, but I had by this time moved up the service scale from nanny to governess and I was about to move up even further. If I had been my father, someone would have said that this was career ambition gone rampant, which it surely was. All the signs were there. At long, long last I had notched my 'governess' credential onto my belt. One step up again! (My God, is there no stopping these Barnards!) Barbara, who had very often come to my aid and pointed me in the right direction, had her boys at the Monterey Pre-Primary School. She said there was a post going there. I applied for it and I got it.

This new rich phase of my life, following my calling and working as a proper teacher with a class of children to call my own for as long as they were in my care, had begun.

~

Later in life, after I'd done a stint in the fashion business, I turned back to teaching. I wanted to teach in the 'special' class for children with problems. I found a relief post as a special teacher but when a permanent appointment was made I applied and didn't get the job.

'Don't worry about it,' Kobus said. (I was married to him by that time.) 'If that's what you want to do, you need to get qualified to do it.'

So I did. I studied for my remedial teacher's qualification by correspondence and it took me two years. I heard I had passed while I was in China, at a conference with Kobus, who is an academic teaching economics and entrepreneurial skills. I had made another step toward my goal and I was in business!

~

I taught in the special class at a school called St Agnes in Woodstock, a working-class suburb of Cape Town. The principal of the school is a wonderful nun called Sister Justina and I just loved teaching there.

Many of the children I taught came from what are described as disadvantaged homes. There were others who came from abusive homes and were living in places of care like *Die Plek* (The Place). I loved them all. I would pile them all into a Kombi and we would go for our lessons to Pick 'n Pay to do my shopping. I would give them each a list and R50 and we'd shop. Then we'd go through the till points and pay for our goods and they would come back to my house to unpack the groceries and work out what our change would be.

Then they'd jump in the swimming pool, have a good time and something nice to eat and drink, and I'd pile them all into the Kombi again and we'd go back to school.

The St Agnes parents were wonderful too. They were the most caring parents you could ever wish to meet. For the most part they had very little money but they simply poured out love onto their children.

And I loved those children. They were simple and direct and it was a great joy to work with them. They were very spontaneous and natural and did things you wouldn't expect.

For example, one day one of my small students took hold of my hand and pulled at the loose skin on the back of my palm and seemed quite alarmed. 'Yussus, Missus,' he said. 'Missus' skin won't go back.' So much for growing old gracefully!

Another child was reading aloud to me and he also came up with the 'Yussus, Missus,' which was a favoured form of address. He thought he'd been reading quite long enough. 'You make me read for a long time,' he said accusingly. Perhaps 'a little learning' suited him just fine and he didn't mind letting me know it!

I had kept all my own children's toys. Even while they were growing up I knew how I'd miss them and I thought one day maybe I'd start a crèche or something like that, and the toys would come in handy. Also, it was a good excuse for not letting them go. But at least in this case there was a practical aim so that hopefully I wouldn't be just another sentimental mother who knows in advance how much she is going to miss her children's childhood days and fears how hard it will be one day to set them free.

I watched those St Agnes children working with those toys, especially the dolls, and the sweetness and goodness of it nearly broke my heart. It's a sad thing to see a child who has been rescued from abuse teach a doll with such tenderness. Watching the St Agnes children in Dolls' Corner was a life lesson from which we could all have benefited.

I have the greatest admiration for the hard-pressed parents at St Agnes and what they try to do for their children. Sometimes they are people who only just manage to hold onto their dignity with their fingernails, but they do it, and that is such an important thing in life, and a gift each of us can give.

I buy at least ten copies of *The Big Issue* every month. I have eye contact and a word for every vagrant and street person who comes my way, and as we all know, there are a great many of them. Each one comes from somewhere. Each one has a story. Sometimes I feel that in my own life and in my own travels and searches, I have felt some kind of sisterhood with them and am closer to them than those people I meet in more rarefied atmospheres.

To have a word, to meet someone's eyes, is to show that we recognise them as people and not just as an irritating and unwanted presence that clutters up space that is rightfully ours. Turning away from them is easy. But turning towards them is easy as well. It's always a sadness to me that so many people find it so difficult.

I've taught at affluent schools too, at schools where the children have 'everything'. They don't even have to share a teacher. If they have a problem they get a one-on-one consultation and then, once the problems are clarified, they are referred out to any one of a very large number of excellent and expensive practitioners. There is nothing money can buy that these children can't have. Sometimes their lives are so cluttered with people trying to help them that they tend to forget what the problems are in the first place.

I can tell you. These are children coping with divorce; with absent parents who have other calls on their time. These are children fobbed off with all those things that money can buy but who are absolutely crying out for love and hands-on parental attention.

At poor schools like St Agnes, the children and parents are anxious to help. They help each other and they can't wait to help you because in their view you are helping their children get a leg up in life. They help in small ways. They'll carry parcels for you; they'll walk with you; they'll carry books. They always have a word and invariably there's a smile. They make time to speak to you. They are always anxious about what their children are doing. They are profuse with thanks and with gratitude when neither is required.

Too often the poor children at affluent schools are dropped off by parents in a hurry or by hired staff. They have all the latest gadgets, everything that money can buy. They know how to talk, they know how to act confident, but the spontaneity is gone and so is the care. They walk through their little lives in shoes that don't have newspaper in them to keep out the rain, that haven't been fixed by their fathers at home, and they see nothing except what they're expected to see and they are truly alone.

I have had other children in my life too.

In the early days of my married life Kobus and I lived in Durban. I taught there at Addington Primary School.

His name was Mark. He was a lovely child and needy. He lived with his mother in a room in Point Road with nothing but one blanket. His mother had a problem with alcohol and I think she may have been a prostitute.

He attached himself to Kobus and me and we were happy to have him, even though we knew that we had to be careful in such circumstances. We had no children of our own in those days and one cannot become too proprietorial, although sometimes it's hard. Mark was in and out of our lives for quite a long time and then our careers moved us to Cape Town. It was difficult. We tried to make it better, for him and for us, by saying that we would send for him, that he could have lovely holidays in Cape Town with us.

We did send for him. A friend of ours, Rael Kaplan, who knew about Mark, offered to pay his air ticket down and he came to spend a holiday with us, but it wasn't the same. The old easiness between us had gone. His coming on holiday – as opposed to moving in and out of our home as he'd been used to doing – changed the dynamic. He was growing up too and changing in that way children do as they get older. Looking back at it now, I suppose he was honing his survival skills. He was still the same lovely boy we had known but he was getting warier and more street-smart.

We were changing too. We'd started our own family. Our life was very full and we drifted away from Mark, although we talked about him sometimes and wondered what had happened to him.

One day, a very long time after, I had a call from the Constantia School for Boys, a school for juvenile offenders just outside Cape Town. Someone wanted to speak to me. It was Mark. 'I don't suppose you remember me,' he said. I did remember him. I remembered him very clearly and I told him so.

It occurred to me afterwards that perhaps he was allowed to make just one telephone call and he decided to telephone me. I don't know. What I do know is that he called just to say that no matter what had happened to him subsequently, he had always remembered his time with Kobus and me.

It was such a sad phone call. The last time I 'saw' Mark was in a photograph on *Police File*, a police television programme that tried to track down people the police were looking for.

I have some 'causes' I care very much about. Street children are a special concern of mine and so is the Masikhule children's home at Crossroads informal settlement outside Cape Town.

I have already mentioned that my father didn't mind treading on toes, official or otherwise, to get things done if it was in a good cause, and in that way I am similar. People who know me will tell you that I have no pride at all when it comes to begging donations from them to help children in need. And I would call myself anything a potential donor might respond to if I thought it might help raise money for them.

I have 'cold-called' I can't tell you how many corporations and anyone who's ever done this will tell you the response you can expect. When Mrs Visser, which is who I am in real life, telephones, the Public Affairs Manager is in a permanent meeting. When I say 'permanent' I mean 'permanent', as in 'remaining indefinitely'; 'indefinitely', as in 'without clearly marked outlines or limits' (thank you, *Chambers Twentieth Century Dictionary*!). Poor things, I hope they at least give them tea and push a *stukkie vetkoek* under the door every now and then just for them to *kou* on – just a small piece of *vetkoek* to keep them going. If you do manage to get hold of them the budget is always 'fully committed'.

When Deirdre Barnard phones, it's a different story. At least she gets put through or her call gets returned.

Henna, who helps out in my house a few mornings a week, didn't like it at first. I'd be on the telephone being Deirdre Barnard, begging with no shame at all for money, and when I had finished she'd wait a while, then she'd say, 'I see you have two names now.' In the beginning she was what you might call slightly acerbic about it.

In the community she comes from, respectable married women don't have two names. They use their husband's name and that's the end of the story and although my husband's name is my pride and my refuge and the place I draw all my strength from, it doesn't raise as much money as having once been Deirdre Barnard does.

So, ek gebruik dit so 'n bietjie. I make use of it occasionally.

I have no illusions about it and in a perfect world perhaps the drop of a well-known name wouldn't count for anything, but in this world it does. If you stop and are absolutely quiet for a moment you can hear all kinds of names being dropped all around you practically every minute of the day. Name dropping happens especially when people want something, and the things I want in life are always for children.

In my adult life I have been given a great deal by children. I have learnt a lot from them, my own included, and I am beginning, just beginning, to hope that maybe they have learnt a little bit from me and their father too.

Last year my free-spirited daughter Karen brought home an eight-year-old street child she'd befriended at the Long Street restaurant where she was working. 'I couldn't just leave him naked in the street getting beaten up,' she said.

She brought him home and took him in. He was an engaging child and he seemed to be happy enough in his new environment. I suppose he liked a clean bed and three decent meals a day. He certainly loved watching television, which was a rare treat for him. Animated cartoons held a special fascination for him and he kept asking for a channel on which one was showing.

I got him into school and hoped he would adjust there as well, but I had learnt from experience that although this all seems a rosy enough picture, the truth is that the lure of the streets always remains extremely seductive to these children. All the same, I had hopes.

I would like to tell you there was a happy ending to the story. The truth is that one day the child disappeared and took Karen's roller blades with him. She saw him back in his old haunts and he never returned to us.

Such things grieve me.

Karen's street child was not the first child outside our family to be taken into our home. When I was a child we had a domestic worker called Lizzie. We met Lizzie on our holidays at Hentie's in Knysna, and when she came to Cape Town she worked for us at our Zeekoevlei house. In due course she had a son and he was named for my brother Andre. Lizzie didn't see fit to confide the name of his father to us, but that made no difference. Lizzie was a part of our household and my second Andre, as I think of him, became a part of it too. There was no question that it could be any other way. He grew up with us, always the son of his mother, but also a son and brother in our house. Lizzie fell victim to alcoholism and that wasn't easy for Andre. Also, apartheid was at its height in those days and I suppose what we were asking him to do was to live in two worlds – and somehow, he did.

My mother can make anything possible. If she accepts someone into her life and takes them under her wing, it's a brave person and a very brave system that tells her she may not! At that time most places were 'Whites Only', including the restaurant in the old Stuttafords department store in Adderley Street, where we liked to go for breakfast sometimes on a Saturday morning for a treat. And of course when we went, second Andre came too. My mother would walk in with her head high and bustle us along and ignore all those looks from white people who weren't quite sure what they should do.

My mother simply sailed on, as if she neither noticed nor cared. I brought up the rear and I was a bit nervous. Years before, when I had been a pupil in Minneapolis, my brother and I had been the butt of jokes about our funny accents. We'd come home crying and my mother, of course, had found our tormentor and asked him what it was all about.

As it turned out, the child involved was not only a bully but also a coward. He told me mother his name was 'Davy Crockett'. She duly noted it down, went in to 'have a word' and got, as one might expect, precisely nowhere.

I learnt, as I'm afraid all children must, how hard it is to be used as a whipping boy for something you have no control over. I didn't want that to happen to second Andre. I wouldn't want it to happen to any child anywhere, whether I knew them or not, but unfortunately the world is rarely that kind.

When he was sixteen I was, in fact, part of an incident that involved second Andre. He and Kobus and I were down in the Waterfront area of Cape Town. Not the smart Waterfront the tourists so enjoy visiting today, but the harbour in the days before it got its facelift.

The Cape Town Festival was on and the three of us went to join in a Bierfest – one of those occasions where everyone sits at long tables drinking beer and dancing to an 'oompah' band. Andre had bought my daughter (then a little girl) a tin moneybox as a gift. He'd handed it over, unwrapped, for us to give to Karen when we went home. It stood on the table between us.

Kobus asked me to dance and while we were dancing Andre sat where he was, sipping his beer and minding his own business, when I saw out of the corner of my eye that something was going on. In our absence Andre had been approached by a white man who'd come up to him, said something I couldn't hear, picked up the money box and squashed it flat the way men like that sometimes squash empty beer tins. Just show what big guys they are.

I was over there in a flash asking him what he thought he was doing. He said what he was doing was putting Andre in his place. He didn't like his attitude. He was acting too white and white men of that kind don't like that, so he'd come just to show him who was boss.

I was furious. I grabbed him by the front of his shirt and told him to apologise right there and then. I think it was the last thing he expected and I can hardly blame him for that. It was the last thing I expected too! I demanded that he apologise to Andre immediately and he did mumble some kind of pathetic apology and then sort of sidled away and that was the end of the Cape Town Festival for us.

I telephoned the mayor's office and let off some steam. Cape Town didn't need 'festivals' if they were going to be festivals like that, which bred incidents like the one we'd been exposed to. The mayor phoned back and apologised, but an apology can take you only so far.

It was sad for all of us to live in a country where you couldn't even sit down quietly, minding your own business, and have a beer with a friend.

I suppose it's just as well Andre and I never got around to dancing together! One woman who did that – it was with Chief Buthelezi at a very highbrow function, as it happens – ended up on the front page of the newspaper. She was lucky. She could have ended up in front of a magistrate.

As we grew up – and my brother Andre, my second Andre and I went through our various ups and downs – the bond with my second Andre held fast and remained strong. He grew up to be a remarkable man. He has a B Tech in Public Administration and a Master's Degree in Human Resources Development and is on the National Board of the Hospice Association of South Africa.

He is, in the eyes of the world, what is termed a success, but he is far more than that. He's a good and kind man in his personal life. He's thoughtful. When I was going through a bad patch in my life I received an enormous bouquet of flowers from him and a card to say he was thinking of me and that I would always have his support. He was there when my brother died, and when my father died he drove to Beaufort West for the funeral.

I see I have gone on for a very long time about children. I think we should all go on for a very long time about children, because adults so often tend to forget that children are very low down in the pecking order. They are truly the voiceless among us and we tend to forget that it's our job, as the forerunners and the adults, to know what their needs are and see that they are attended to.

People have asked me if I care so much about the voicelessness of children because I have had my own experience of voicelessness. I have already touched on this topic earlier in a different way, but I think they mean in the matter of being heard by my parents, primarily my father. The fact is that I found training for waterskiing very hard, but to achieve at international level is a hard thing to do. My father was greatly pleased by my achievements, that's quite true, but so was I. I liked to be an achiever and although sometimes it made me weep bitter tears, I knew very well that this was the price of success. Could I have protested? Yes, I could, but I didn't. Is this the same as finding myself 'voiceless' – wanting to stop the competitive skiing but not saying so because I so badly wanted to please my father? No, I don't think so, because there were days when I was perfectly happy to do all that was required of me and on those other days something inside me, perhaps that 'hard-headedness' I spoke of before, made me continue. I might have said at many times in my life that I'd had enough, especially when I found myself powerless in the face of the press having its picnic with my family, but that is not the person I am. I talk a very great deal and chirp up when I feel indignant and want to make myself heard, but deep down inside myself the person I am is the kind who keeps silent and simply carries on. That isn't being silenced, it's simply me.

I am going to tell you the greatest thing I ever learnt from a child, and he was a very tiny baby, not more than four or five months old.

Kobus and I were driving up Upper Buitengracht Street in Cape Town. It's an inner-city area. There are a great many street people there. You see them with their trolleys and their bottles of cheap wine or methylated spirits. Sometimes in winter when it's cold you see them under the flyovers, hunched over whatever kind of fire they've managed to scrape together.

On this day, on an island in the middle of the road, lay a very drunk woman. She held up in her arms a tiny baby of four or five months. The child was wearing only a nappy and the rain was torrential. She lay there on her back, drunk, throwing the baby up in the air and then catching it again. Up it went and down, with its tiny legs sticking out of its nappy and the rain pouring down.

I couldn't believe what I was seeing. I was filled with an indescribable feeling of pain and of anger. I could feel something inside me just fall apart.

I shouted to Kobus to stop. I started screaming. 'Stop! Stop! Stop!'

He got such a fright that he did stop, he stopped in such a hurry that the car actually mounted the pavement and I was out of it across the street like a flash.

That is a busy road. There are cars going up and down all the time. Sometimes, in rush hour, there are traffic jams. There was no traffic jam that day, but the road was busy. Affluent people, in nice cars, muffled up in warm clothes, with heaters on and radios playing, must have seen what I saw. No one else stopped.

'Call the police!' I shouted to Kobus.

I took hold of the baby and pulled the drunk mother up to her feet the best way I could, and the cars came and went and the rain just kept coming down.

'Call the police!' I kept shouting, while Kobus was on the mobile phone doing just that.

Somehow I got the woman to the side of the road where her trolley with all her worldly goods in it was standing. I had a warm coat on and I tried to tuck the baby inside it to get it warm, but the baby wouldn't budge. That child clung to its mother the way those tiny little monkeys hang on for dear life under their mothers because that is all the security they know.

I stood there in the rain crying, waiting for the police to come, with a woman so drunk she was like someone from another planet.

This tiny rain-soaked baby, who had barely known anything of this world, clung fast to its mother, and it seemed to me as I stood there as if I was powerless. As if there was no force that was strong enough to prise it away.

In Buitengracht Street, Cape Town, on a cold winter day, I stood in the rain and I wept because I knew what was in that child's heart. This was his mother. This was the person he loved. In my heart I understood it. I understood it in my bones. It was really very simple and also unbearably sad.

Even when they got into the police van to be taken away to be 'dealt with' by social services, that child still clung on for dear life and that was how I saw him go. I couldn't stop it. I couldn't change it.

I knew then what I had always known. Love is a mysterious thing. That's simply the way it is.

16

Divorce

'The family unit is the basis of the nation.' [My father, 1992]

*'Divorce is bad for children. My family is everything
to me. I would fight tooth and nail to keep my
family together.'* [Me. Any day you care to ask me]

I come from a family which values service to the community, and as
children tend to follow their parents, I suppose it's hardly surprising
that my brother wanted to be a veterinary surgeon before deciding
to become a doctor. When I went to university in my first year I
enrolled to do social science because I wanted to be a social worker.

My father, before his arthritis prevented him practising hands-
on, worked at Groote Schuur, which is a state hospital. This is not
a place where you work if you want to make a great deal of money.
If that is your goal then private practice in a good part of town is
where you want to be.

Guy de Cauliac (1300–1370) said the following:

Let the Surgeon be bold in all sure things and fearful in
dangerous things; let him avoid all faulty treatment and
practices.

He ought to be gracious to the sick, considerate to his
associates, cautious in his prognostications.

> Let him be modest, dignified, gentle, pitiful and merciful;
> not covetous nor an extortionist of money; but rather let his
> reward be according to his work, to the means of his
> patient, to the quality of his issue and to his own dignity.

I know many people thought my father fell down in the modesty department and that he wasn't perhaps as dignified as they'd have liked, that he liked to dance, play the ukulele and have a good time. I know there are some of his associates who will say with a grunt that he could very often be less than gracious, but he felt genuine pity for people in need, and he was gentle. Anyone who had ever seen his approach to a sick child will tell you that. He was definitely not an extortionist. Anyone who had been privy to his pay slips in the early days or the pension payments at the end of his life could have confirmed this.

My mother, who worked so hard to supplement the family income, would be happy to give you more details. She would also confirm what he said of himself, which is that he 'wasn't focused on family life'. As his career pressures increased, those old carefree days became a thing of the past. I think we all knew it. I think deep down inside ourselves we knew something else too, which was that he wouldn't ever come back again.

Many things drove my father, sometimes at great cost to those closest to him. He knew this and said so, but one thing he was never driven by was money.

Someone reminded me of that the other day and it's quite true: my father never levied any charge for treating people. He'd been given certain skills and they were available to anyone who needed them and in these days of the quick buck, how many people do you know who can truly make the same claim?

The profits from his first book, *One Life*, were donated towards the building of a heart centre at the University of Cape Town. The centre was very important to him. He was rather starry-eyed in those days, and I think he had a vision of Cape Town and Groote Schuur being some kind of mecca where specialists and researchers from all over the world could come to pool their knowledge and exchange ideas.

Despite all the glamour that surrounded him, he was first and foremost a doctor. The driving force of his life was to be able to use his skills to improve the quality of life of his patients and help alleviate the misery of the human condition where he could.

As Bob Molloy pointed out later,

> The Barnard charisma, beamed out at countless after-dinner speaking engagements and in tireless speaking tours of America and Europe, was bringing in cash. He worked as if driven, carrying a punishing workload sandwiched between barnstorming appearances at international conferences, jetting from continent to continent on the fund-raising trail.

Another reporter remarked that the new heart centre building at Medical School was costing 'an arm and a leg'. Bob Molloy's opinion was that it cost my father a great deal more than that. It cost him 'his health, two marriages and most of his working life', and I think that's quite true.

I also wanted to do something with my life that would be of some use to others, not to follow in my father's footsteps, but to do something for myself. My first choice was social work, which was a good choice for me, but my timing was wrong. When I started university, the year after I'd done my year as a professional water-skier, which I suppose these days one would call a gap year, our life as a family was drawing to an end, and it was a very sad end.

My father has written that he and my mother were 'living like strangers'. It was something my brother and I could hardly avoid noticing. There were tensions and there was a sinking, apprehensive feeling, but even so nobody discussed the possibility of divorce – at least, they didn't with us. I suppose because that was a different generation and it was just the way we were brought up.

One day, when my mother was driving me to school, she told me she was going to divorce my father. I knew about divorce but I didn't understand the mechanics of it. At that time, when my father was in the country, he was living at 'home' in our house in Zeekoevlei. He still had a front door key and there was no sound in the world as wonderful to me as to hear that key turn in the lock when my father came back from wherever it was he had been. It meant Pappa's home, the circle's complete, we are still a family; but it couldn't continue.

Have you ever had that feeling of 'the last time'? There are some things in your life you think will go on forever, then one day it's the 'last time' – only, while it's happening, it seems just like every other time, and so you don't know that this is in fact the very last time. When you look again, it's all over.

During that time, my father and I still went out on the lake occasionally, but he had little time for it now. He was busy with his new life and all the commitments that came along with it. I was coming to the end of my skiing days and we both knew it.

> My daughter, Deirdre, and I had been very close over the past five years – in fact until the transplant, I had focused most of my attention on her. Her achievements in waterskiing were major highlights in my life.

He and I never talked about the divorce or its implications.

My parents had been married for twenty years. On the day their divorce was finalised in the Cape Town Supreme Court, my father was in Majorca. There was no requirement for him to be physically present when the final decree was granted. All the same, he said it was a sad day for him.

I relived the day when I first saw her as a patient in a ward for sick nurses, the reception after our wedding, my getting sunburnt on our honeymoon. How sad that it all had to end like this.

He recognised also that his divorce from my mother was to have the most profound effect on several lives, 'especially those of my children'.

At that time Andre in his last year of school, was about to join the navy for his national service and Deirdre was at university. A divorce like the one we were headed for is very tough on the children.

Andre told me that he had heard about it for the first time when he was coming out of school one afternoon. He read about our separation on the newspaper poster in big bold print. Who can ever quantify the effects of such shocking news to a boy that age?

The children of divorce are frightened and frequently depressed. Even though the parents may be concerned they are seldom able to provide sufficient help or emotional support. In our children's case it was made much worse by the wide publicity the proceedings attracted.

My father was not very proud of the fact that he had failed to keep any of his three marriages together. He believed in the family unit and hated divorce. He said: 'Families represent major inputs of love, time and labour – dozens of working years invested by parents, children and other relations.'

Do you think it's strange that he placed such value on the family unit? I don't. My father, like most interesting people, was full of contradictions. He made mistakes but he never tried to deny them. Perhaps he will not be remembered for being the perfect parent, but I really do believe he loved his children and did his best for them.

He paid for all my university education and my brother's, although my brother got monetary concessions because of my father's connection with the University of Cape Town. Many of our peers were there on scholarships, some of them because their parents believed 'coming up the hard way' was good for young people – another good old Calvinist trait that's probably done more harm than good, but my father didn't subscribe to it. He wanted his children to be the best they could be and he was willing to give them the foundation on which they could build.

During that year that led up to my parents' divorce I was not yet at university; I was still waterskiing. My mother had dropped the 'one shoe' of my parents' forthcoming divorce. The 'second shoe' was finding out that it was a *fait accompli* from a newspaper placard while I was at the South African Games in Bloemfontein (see Chapter 8).

Our family, as I've told you, are not the world's best communicators. Also, they come from a long tradition in which certain subjects are taboo and not for public discussion, and in the case of divorce, certainly not for discussion with children.

Just after the divorce my father was in Europe once more. He'd been to Madrid, where General Franco had honoured him with the Blue Cross, and was on his way to St Tropez.

He came to see me in Copenhagen, where I was getting ready to take part in the European waterskiing championships.

It wasn't a good time. My father said:

> My heart went out to my daughter. She was not with her father any more, she wasn't skiing well and worst of all, she was considerably overweight. I realised then how a physical defect visible to others could cause so much suffering.

I took Deirdre shopping and bought her some clothes that would hide the bulges. She pleaded with me to stay on but I was drawn like a magnet back to St Tropez.

My father's life in South Africa had changed a very great deal since he'd moved out of our lives in the Zeekoevlei house. He now had a far more glittering arrangement in Clifton, the millionaire strip of the Atlantic seaboard. A friend, Gila Krugel, had offered him the use of an apartment in a block called La Corniche. It had been some time since I'd last heard the grating of his key in the lock at Zeekoevlei. I understood the way things were now, but it hurt.

Afterwards, I read that he had said that 'coming home after an overseas trip is always a joyous experience, an inner glow, a feeling of elation that lasts for days'.

That was how it was for me when he came home. That's how I felt when I heard his key turn in the lock at our old family home, but I don't think it was only our Zeekoevlei home he was writing about. He was nostalgic for our last sad days as a family as well. Not that this alters anything.

My young life was dominated by my father. I looked like him, I thought I was like him. We shared waterskiing. I considered him 'mine' and thought myself special to him, in a way. It was only afterwards that I realised that while I was taking up so much of his time and allowing him to fill my life the way he did, my brother, who was different from me and whose interests were different from mine, was losing out.

My brother was a nice, normal boy, pleasant to look at, with a good sense of humour, extremely gifted in some areas, just about average in others. Which is to say he was just the same as the rest of us.

The trouble is that I am not quite sure how easy it is to be 'normal' and stay that way when you happen to find yourself in a family like ours.

My brother could waterski too, but he did it for pleasure. He wasn't a public performer like I was. He was good, though, and he was kind. In my year of skiing overseas he and my mother were invited to Spain by an industrialist called Mr Barreoros and he was kind enough to include me in the invitation.

They were staying at La Toga and they sent a private jet to fetch me in London. I suppose they'd been talking about my skiing. As hosts, they couldn't do enough for us: I thought it was so kind and so generous of them to make it possible for me to be with my mother and brother again. The last thing I expected to have to do was ski, but when I arrived they'd got all the equipment I needed together, so that I could entertain them with an exhibition. I was meant, I knew, to 'show them what I could do on skis'. It was a simple enough request. It was the story of my life in those days, but I just couldn't do it, not for love or for money, not to please anyone, not to be polite, not for anything at all.

You know that feeling when you just wish the ground would open and swallow you up? That was what I felt. I'd put on huge amounts of weight. I felt so ashamed of myself. The last thing I wanted was to be put on public display. I'm a person who, all of my life, has been anxious to please, but I could not have 'pleased' those people if you paid me a million pounds to do it.

My brother understood this. He knew me. During the divorce, which hadn't been the best time for either of us, he had been very supportive of me.

I was fat, I was lonely and I didn't have a boyfriend. Andre was a medical student at that time and he included me in his crowd and tried to give me some kind of life.

I couldn't have skied at that Barreoros party, not for anything. Yet if I said 'no' I would probably have spent the rest of my life feeling terrible about it, so he simply stepped in and put everything right.

He said I wasn't really up to skiing but he would give them a show instead of me, and he did. He gave a wonderful performance and I think it was even better than my doing it because it was so unexpected. You don't have to win medals or get public accolades to be a sufficiently good skier to give spectators pleasure. In fact, there's something about just getting out there on the water and doing something like skiing, and doing it effortlessly and with pleasure, that I suppose one could, in today's parlance, call 'cool'.

So by that token, my brother was 'cool' then, and he was a great deal more. He bailed me out of a bad place just as he'd had occasion to do sometimes in the past, and our hosts were more than satisfied. Just imagine, more than one Barnard who could water-ski! They had no idea of the other things he could do.

Besides being a skier, he was also a serious surfer and had a pair of knee-pads, the kind surfers wear, except that knee-pads weren't easily available in those days and his were custom-made by my mother (of course) – Ouma Louwtjie's bespoke tailoring again!

Snapshot memories. Wonderful holidays at Buffels Bay and my brother, tanned by the sun, perfect and beautiful in the way young men are beautiful, walking out of the water holding his surfboard, with holiday sounds all around him and everything saturated in sunlight. I like to remember him like this.

He had his quirks. When he was a boy he used to carry a cricket scoring pad around with him and play imaginary cricket games in his head, faithfully noting down the score as the game progressed.

He was happy in his own head and a dreamer. *Loskop*, we called him, which is to say Scatterbrain, but you say it in an affectionate way with a shake of the head, a bit like saying 'Planet Earth calling Andre' because you can see he's miles away in some place of his own. His son Adam, who is so very much like his father to look at, is a bit like that too.

When we were children, when after our great trek by cargo boat and then by plane we eventually managed to join our father in

Minneapolis, he had gifts for us. I got a doll's pram. Andre got a set of plastic cowboys and Indians, and was immediately at home and happy. He started a frontier war at once, of course, and could keep himself busy for hours just lying on the bed pretending he was General Custer or something, playing out his war game with all the appropriate sound effects.

I suppose it was the forerunner of the video games of today. Andre enjoyed it and his sound effects would certainly have had no problem standing the test of time. They were something else!

He liked acquiring information. He was a collector of the *Guinness Book of Records*: each year when the new edition came out he bought it. He loved dipping into encyclopedias and regularly dazzled us by coming out with the most esoteric information you could ever imagine.

Quirky. He was certainly that. We knew him like that and we loved him.

I wanted to do a paper on divorce as one of my projects. Professor Erika Theron, who was one of my lecturers and knew my circumstances, counselled against it. She said it was too close to me, and she was right. In fact, I was not going to do a paper on divorce or on anything else that year. I consistently bunked classes. I didn't do assignments. I spent a lot of time lying in bed. I wanted to sleep. I wanted my old life back.

My mother moved away from Zeekoevlei after my brother graduated. She sold the house to Dolf van der Merwe, who had used to come and whistle outside at six o'clock every morning in all weathers so that he, my father and I could get the boat ready, get out on the vlei and could start practising.

I used to dream about that house. It was the first house my parents owned. My mother's father helped them buy it. I used to dream that I could one day buy it and go back and be there again, even long after I knew it wasn't possible. It wasn't just the house I wanted, it was the life I had had there when I'd been happy. That was gone. I knew that. The child I had been was gone too, consigned to once-upon-a-time land. I knew that too. There was no going back, not physically, not emotionally, no way at all.

That was how things were whether I liked it or not. I knew that very well. It was gone, it was history and I knew it had to be faced. While I tried to sort it all out in my own mind and sum up the courage to face it, I got fat again.

Even now, when I look back, everything else recedes and that stands out. When my father eventually moved out of Zeekoevlei and we no longer heard the sound of his key turning in the lock, he moved not only to a different address but also into a different, far more glittering world.

It was difficult for us. I had been a child of immense privilege. A great fuss had been made of me because of my waterskiing. I'd been taken out of school many times so I could concentrate on my skiing. I had travelled a great deal all over the world and in my own country people recognised me on the streets as some kind of watery prodigy.

I hope I wasn't too proud, but I wasn't like other girls my age. In fact, I wasn't quite sure what other girls my age were actually like at all. I suppose there was some kind of hubris involved, and as we all know, hubris actually invites disaster and disaster was coming my way soon enough.

I had always felt as if my father had somehow singled me out. I had thought that what made us special was that we were such a good team. I really had moments when I was on a high, when there was the 'rush' of having won and the slightly euphoric feeling that goes with it. It was only later that I realised that, as with everything else in life, this came with a price tag.

It can be very hard when half the world seems to own a bit of your father. It was hard for my brother and it was hard for me.

Sometimes you look back and wonder what's left over that's entirely personal to you. My strongest memory of my father, in that time when he stood at the very centre of my world, is at Hentie's Botel in Knysna. The skiers at the hotel were giving a show and my brother was in it. He was one of the seven dwarfs.

That particular day, which was actually quite ordinary, stands out like a beacon in my mind. Perhaps because it fixes us all so firmly in our places in that time where we believed our entire life would be made up of days exactly like that.

Would I freeze-frame that day if I could, the way that they do on TV? The answer, of course, must be no; or maybe yes, but just for a moment, because real life's not like TV and I wouldn't want it to be. There are few things in life that are predictable. The one thing that is, whether we like it or not, is that life rolls along on its own course and there's not very much we can do to stop it.

My father's glamorous new world among the rich and well-travelled people who gravitated toward his apartment in La Corniche didn't seem to hold too many attractions for Andre. It did for me. I loved the flashiness of it. I wanted to be a part of it, even though to do so meant undergoing a kind of sea change as you moved from one world into another that was so very different. I was willing to do it. I considered myself adaptable and believed I could succeed.

I am quite sure this hurt my mother. I think very often, now that I am older, how very much my mother was taken for granted in so many ways. She had supplied a safe haven and stable childhood for Andre and me. For a great deal of our growing up life, because of my father's work, she was a single parent. We couldn't imagine it any other way. She worked and provided financial security. Isn't that what parents are supposed to do for their children? We thought it was.

When my father found himself in the bright lights and the pressures became unbearable and they divorced, my mother was meant to be strong about that as well. After all, had she not always been the strong one? Why should this be any different?

I don't think I made it any easier. I wanted to continue to be a part of my father's life. She said if that's what I wanted then that's what I must do. As I've already said, I knew what she said and what she thought were two very different things, but I did what I wanted anyway. She knew that I would.

Andre was different. I suppose in his way, he was more sensitive to my mother's needs, more willing to acknowledge what was left unsaid, more inclined to feel responsible for her happiness at this hard time in her life than I'd been. I know how I felt, but I was pushier and a quick and sometimes rash decision-maker. Of course I could feel the maelstrom of emotions that whirled around the fact of my parents parting from each other and divorcing. I wanted to push my way through all of that and even if I had to have my parents separately, I wanted to salvage any part of the old life that I could.

It wasn't so easy for my brother. He took upon himself a greater burden of the turmoil that buffeted both our lives in those days.

My brother was very good-looking and pleasant to be with, and there were always people happy to be in his company, yet I sensed an aloneness in him. He was my brother less than a year apart from me in age, and yet he was at a distance from me. It hurt me to see it. It was like watching him standing alone on an ice floe with the sea all around him. I wanted to hold out my hand and ask him to take that single step that would bring him back, but I didn't know how to do it.

Even then I had a feeling that he was beginning to move away from us, and even if all of us who loved him so much reached out to him he would not be able to take hold of our hands.

My brother finished his schooling in Pretoria, where he stayed with Martin and Kitty Franzot, who were very good friends of my parents. I think my mother thought it would be good for him to be 'rooted' in the nice down-to-earth kind of environment she preferred. It's what she'd always provided for us, but that was becoming an increasingly hard thing to offer in that run up to the divorce and the period while it was all actually happening.

My father, by his own admission, 'had always been close to Deirdre but Andre had unfortunately taken a back seat'. I think my mother read this situation very well and as usual tried to do the best thing she could for Andre.

So she made her decision to send Andre to stay with family friends in Pretoria. It is not something my mother would have done casually. She was far too good and caring a parent for that. I love my mother but I cannot read her heart. My own feeling is that this was a decision that came at considerable personal cost, but she did it anyway. Where my brother and I are concerned our best interests were always her major concern.

Andre was very fond of these 'surrogate parents' and when Martin Franzot became very ill and went into heart failure he telephoned my father to ask for his help. My father responded at once because that's the way it still was. As far as my brother and I were concerned, when there was a crisis and we really needed him there was never such a thing as having to take a back seat. He was there, no questions asked. We knew if there was one thing we could depend on, it was that, and this time was no exception.

Martin was 52 years old – two years older than the cut-off date decided on for potential new heart recipients. All the same, my father told Andre to get Martin to Cape Town and he'd see what he could do, and he did. He flouted the rules and got Martin the operation he so desperately needed to survive, but on this occasion there was no miracle to be had. Martin Franzot died.

My father tried to explain it to Andre, who must have been devastated. Andre loved Martin as if he were his own father and his own father, whom the whole world seemed to look to for miracles, had no miracle to offer him.

My father explained that the new, transplanted heart couldn't carry enough of the circulation to keep him alive. I think it must have been very hard for him to tell Andre this. I don't think he was as close to Andre as he would have liked to be, or felt he should have been.

I am convinced that nothing would have gratified my father more than to have been able to help Martin Franzot. But Andre, I suppose, was angry in the way that one can become irrationally angry in the face of the death of someone you love.

'Why didn't you put back his old heart, then?' he wanted to know. 'At least that kept him alive.'

I think my father and my brother were both upset. Certainly my father said afterwards that the whole business troubled him. He couldn't sleep. While he lay awake with my brother's words still ringing in his ears, he came to a decision. He felt sure that if the patient's old heart had been left in place to give what support it could to the new heart, Martin Franzot would still have been alive. He decided to pursue the idea of the heterotopic heart transplant, the piggyback heart.

In his own way my father did try to reach out to Andre and 'make magic' for him in the way he had always done for me.

He knew Andre was mad about *The Goon Show* and when Peter Sellers came to South Africa and asked if he could watch heart surgery being performed, my father accommodated his request.

My father introduced Andre to Peter Sellers. He and Barbara were newly moved into Waiohai then and she gave a party for him so that Andre and a group of his friends could meet the famous British comedian. Peter Sellers didn't let them down. They all sat down on the floor and he kept them in fits of laughter for the entire evening.

When Andre made the decision to do medicine it pleased my father enormously. He felt it would give them something in common and draw them closer together. He said that as he came to know my brother as an adult, he 'gave me a lot of pleasure'. When my father retired Andre, who was then practising as a paediatrician at Red Cross Children's Hospital, was there to see him being given a commemorative gift.

Something else that made him very happy was that Andre did better in his exams at Medical School than my father himself had ever done. My father always valued achievement, so this pleased him enormously.

But things were not well with my brother, although on the surface his life appeared to go on much as usual without any cause for concern.

He met Gail, an English nursing sister and a very capable young woman, and they were married in England.

My father treated them to a holiday in Greece and Kobus and I spent as much time with them as we could. In that way our life as a family continued and is dotted with those occasions and milestones you take so for granted at the time, and remember with such tenderness afterwards.

There was the announcement of new babies on the way, Ashlea and Adam for Gail and Andre; Karen and Tiaan for Kobus and me. There were the christening parties that followed. There were suppers and braais and gatherings with my mother's family at the farm Keurweerder at Paarl, and the children beginning to grow up and our lives moving on.

I never questioned that my brother, so close to me in age, and I would go on into old age together. After all, that's the natural progression, isn't it? We grow up, grow old and hopefully live to see our children happy and enjoy our grandchildren. Parents die before their children and no one dies young. We all live out our appointed span with enough time left over to look back and see the entire story of the thing we call our life that we leave in our wake. Of course, it isn't quite so simple.

I can remember clearly the morning I was told that my brother was dead. We were telephoned and told that there had been 'an accident'.

You know, that kind of phone call we all dread? The solemn voice says 'there's been an accident'. Your heart starts to sink like lead before you even hear the end of the sentence because somewhere at the very centre of all that you are, you know exactly what it is that's coming next.

Kobus, always good in a crisis, got things together and we went to my brother's house absolutely filled with foreboding, expecting something really terrible but not quite knowing exactly what it was that we expected.

I was desperately afraid of what we might find. My brother, I knew, had been deeply unhappy, plagued by the kind of despair none of us seemed able to find any cure for.

He and I were very different in temperament. I realise now that because of the direction in which his own life had borne him, he had in a sense missed out on a crucial phase of his growing-up. He had, by his own choice, assumed a man's role when he was really no more than a boy. I suppose in a sense you could say he had an old-fashioned view of the world: he thought men should protect women and ensure they were taken care of. He loved my mother and wanted with all his heart to make things better, when apart from just going on being the truly loving son he was, he really had no power to do so.

He was protective of me too. He used to reprimand me if he thought it was necessary. If I tried to sneak in long after midnight after some party or other he'd be waiting for me, demanding an explanation in the way a father might have done. He was too young to assume such a responsibility. Yet he did, and the cost to himself was that he missed out on a certain *joie de vivre* that other young people enjoyed.

As a teacher I am very aware that there are certain clearly defined phases a small child must go through. I seem very often to ask: 'Did the child crawl?' I ask because it's important. During the crawling phase the child learns to gauge distances and establish spatial relationships. All through our growing-up lives we go through a chain of learning curves, the success of each link dependent on how successfully we managed to conquer its predecessor.

It seemed as if joy evaded my brother, who was always so willing to take on responsibilities, even when they had long since become almost unbearable burdens. Yet life gave him gifts too. He had everything in Gail, the most wonderful wife, mother, daughter and sister-in-law anyone could wish for; and he had his two lovely children. But even so the feeling of distance and loneliness I had first felt long ago seemed always now somehow to shroud him, and it disturbed me. My heart was very heavy in those early morning hours when the telephone call, that kind of call we all fear and dread, finally came.

When we arrived the ambulancemen were carrying out a stretcher.

I said: 'Shame, is that my brother, is he hurt?'

They said: 'No, he's dead.'

Just like that. That was how my brother entered the past.

My father was away on another trip, this time as guest lecturer on the *QE2*. When the trip ended he had to go on to London for some work on a TV documentary. He was alone in his hotel room when Fritz Brink telephoned him to tell him that my brother was dead.

My father came home at once. He said it was the saddest journey he'd ever made, and when he arrived in Cape Town the photographers were there waiting for him, those 'gawpers' at the scene of the accident who can do nothing to help but seem to get some voyeuristic pleasure out of moments like this.

'Only doing our job,' is what they would tell you if you asked.

What kind of a job is that? That's what I'd like to know. How does a father feel when his son dies? When one of them can give you the answer to that from personal experience, maybe he or she will also understand that common decency should make certain things sacrosanct, especially from media intrusion. I have no great hope of this happening, though.

The press was at my brother's funeral service. I imagine there was some speculation about who would weep and who would not. Photographers poked long lenses into our faces and into our privacy.

This is a very hard thing to bear. It was a very difficult thing for my brother's wife, Gail, a very dignified woman, the mother of their two small children who, it was decided, would not attend the service.

My brother had died tragically in circumstances that required a coroner's report. In itself that was a difficult thing to come to terms with, but it was made worse by the fact that long before this report was made public the media had a field day with all kinds of deeply hurtful speculations.

One reporter, a woman, was particularly vicious. She quoted from a letter my brother had written to my father at the time my parents divorced. He was fifteen years old at the time, bewildered, uprooted and harsh in his criticism of my father.

The divorce hurt all of us. We may have wished it otherwise, we may not have liked it, but we had long since come to terms with it and put it behind us. Now it was all dragged up again. I felt for my parents. I felt for the reporter, a woman who had nothing better to do than give another lash of the whip, as if my brother's death and the nature of it had not been quite enough for my father to bear.

My father had always been tolerant of the press. Many people say he courted them. If that is so then I think you should know that that was the day the courtship ended. Deeply hurt, my father wrote:

> Most destructive was the unlovely soul who dug around in a newspaper file to find a fifteen-year-old point of dissension between me and my dead son and then wrote it into an account of the funeral. All of us at times add to the sum of human unhappiness. Some out of love, some from hate – which is simply the other side of the same coin – and some for profit. The last category is the least forgivable.

As for me, I feel sorry for this poor woman of all those years ago. Having to resort to deliberate cruelty to gain some measure of gratification and self-esteem is a sad thing. Perhaps she was so spiritually impoverished that she needed it at that time. Perhaps all the snide digs about my father and our family in the press were not more or less than the Barnard-hunters' right, and one must allow people to do what they think is right and what pleases them. Some people are like that, but we are not. The Barnards may be many things but no one in our family derives any pleasure from the misery of others. It is simply not our way and it's very hard for us that so much interest surrounds our most private moments.

Some time after my brother died my father was interviewed on the BBC's *Hard Talk* programme. The interviewer was Tim Sebastian. The tone of the interview was light-hearted. Mr Sebastian teased my father about a rather natty waistcoat he was wearing. My father, interviewed so many times, was enjoying it, and I had the feeling that Mr Sebastian, himself no new kid on the block when it came to interviewing, was enjoying himself too.

Usually the topics to be covered are discussed before the show is filmed. This makes for a better interview, but Tim Sebastian has a way of sliding in some unexpected personal question – I suppose because it livens things up and makes for an even better interview. I honestly don't think he asked what he did in order to be deliberately hurtful. I am perfectly sure that he didn't expect the response his question occasioned.

In an offhand kind of way, Tim Sebastian asked my father how he felt when his son died. Isn't it strange? Personally, I would consider it a hundred times over before I asked even my closest friend such a question because, to my mind, that is how enormously personal it is, but then I am not a famous television interviewer whose life is ordered by ratings.

My father replied very calmly. He spoke of his sadness at putting off a talk he'd been wanting to have with my brother. He had known he was troubled and had wanted to help him. His response was so calm and measured that you would almost have thought the moment had passed and yet, after the question was answered, my father began to weep. It was a terrible thing to see. I couldn't bear to watch. I couldn't look at it without weeping myself for the sadness of it, because I am a part of my father just as my brother was.

It's a strange thing. A child can be delivered of a mother, physically taken out of her body – that is a matter of the flesh. A matter of the blood is something else altogether, and in that way children can never be divided from their parents or from each other. I didn't need my brother's death to remind me of this.

In front of millions of viewers my father wept for my brother, a man unable to contain his grief, his heart breaking for all to see. If you asked me what it was like to be Christiaan Barnard, then I would tell you that is how it was. You might consider this and then ask yourself if, given all the fame, the accolades and the good times, you really would choose to change places.

As for me, people ask me why the death of my father affected me in a way that was different from the death of my brother but then, as I told you, people have asked me a great many things in my life.

The difference, I suppose, is that my father's death, telephoned in by a stranger from such a very long way away, was a very great shock. Although he was an old man, I wasn't ready. I suppose that seems a strange thing to say, so I will qualify it by saying that in many ways I felt as if I had just begun to find again the father I had known in my childhood days. This new lease of life in our relationship was very precious to me. My children were grown up, my heavily hands-on days of mothering were behind me, and I believed there were things I could still do for my father, to make up for lost time if you like.

My brother's death was shocking, but my brother and I had no 'matters outstanding' in the way I felt I had with my father. As I have explained earlier in this book, my brother had Gail, he had his family and the life they had built for themselves. They had a world which I could and did enter, but they were a unit, just as Kobus and I and our children are a unit, and it was that unit, Gail and her children, who stood at the very centre of the loss of my brother.

With my brother, for a very long time I had stood on the sidelines and watched him carrying a terrible sadness inside himself. He had reminded me of Atlas, the man with the world on his shoulders, but with his death that too had ended. I felt it. I felt it so strongly that it was almost as if I could see that great heavy burden simply being lifted from him and Andre being free, walking upright again.

We had a fine member of our household, Sarah, who worked for us and who had seen all those things we had. When she heard of the death of my brother she said to me: '*Die Here vat net vol mandjies op Hemel toe.*' God only takes up a basket to Heaven when it's full.

I liked that. It comforted me. I felt in a special sense that my brother was full to overflowing, that the burden that he carried somewhere at the core of his being had become just too heavy to bear any longer. I think he knew 'the solitary pain that gnaws at the heart'. After his death, even at his funeral, I felt as if a great peace had descended.

I knew no peace when I was told of the death of my father. I felt only pain and there was, for quite a long time, no room for anything else.

Sometimes people, even people who know me quite well, say I am a bit too much of a Mary Sunshine, as if I somehow glide over the surface of things and ignore what lies beneath. The truth is that while I like to share good things and affirm life experiences, I like to keep the sad things to myself. If you believe in old adages, then I am the one who cries alone, and sometimes I've done it with people all around me and without shedding any visible tears at all.

I have, in my life, lost people I love. I have turned to share a thought, an emotion with someone who is no longer there. I have sometimes found myself, on my way home, absent-mindedly driving up the road to where my father's last house stands, and realised that now there's nothing at all but emptiness where there was so much of life going on.

I have, in the full heat of summer, seen a young man walking down a beach and half turned to greet him, before realising that he is not that young man I thought he was. He is not my brother. My brother, had he lived, would have been older now. That young man he was is gone and I have felt a loss so great and a surge of memory so strong that all of my spirit, that thing that sustains me, has creaked beneath the burden of it.

In my life, I've had a great many questions and sometimes rather too few answers, and in this matter of loss, if someone else could speak for me these are the words I would choose.

The *Canon of St Paul's Cathedral in England* was written by Henry Scott Holland, who lived from 1847 to 1918. It says:

> Death is nothing at all. I have only slipped into the next room. I am I, and you are you. Whatever we were to each other, that we still are. Call me by my old familiar name, speak to me in the easy way which you always used. Put no difference in your tone, wear no forced air of solemnity or sorrow. Laugh as we always laughed at the little jokes we enjoyed together. Play, smile, think of me, pray for me. Let my name be ever the household word it always was, let it be spoken without effect, without the trace of a shadow on it. Life means all that it ever meant. It is the same as it ever was; there is unbroken continuity. Why should I be out of mind because I am out of sight? I am waiting for you, for an interval, somewhere very near, just around the corner. All is well.

As regards my father, as regards my brother: 'Whatever we were to each other, that we still are.' There is no power in the world strong enough to change that, and that is my comfort.

17

Get thee to a nunnery

This may sound funny coming from a
Barnard, and I didn't exactly do it,
but it did have its attractions

My Beaufort West grandfather, Adam, was a Dutch Reformed missionary and a very humble man. I think we have something of the missionary in our DNA and in a way it has affected us all.

In the last television interview my father gave in South Africa before his death on *People of the South* with Dali Tambo as interviewer, Dali asked my Dad what the greatest sadness of his life was.

My father was, at that time, a man not unacquainted with sadness in all its many guises. Yet he said that his greatest sadness was that his father had died a month before he performed the first open-heart procedure. 'He was so proud of his children,' my father said. He was always much moved, especially later in his life, when he talked about his father and remembered his simplicity and goodness.

I can understand that. In many ways my father was a complex man, but ultimately we all draw on our background, our memories and our experiences. They are, after all, what make us what we are.

My brother and I were raised in the Dutch Reformed (DR) Church. My parents didn't often go to church but they thought it proper that we should be a part of our community and have suitable religious education.

When we were old enough and at home in South Africa, which is to say excluding our time in Minneapolis, my mother got us all togged up in the beautiful clothes she made for us, and off we went to Sunday School.

In the DR Church in those days you got points for attending church. You had a little book and the teacher put stamps in it. For a long time in my life I thought about that little book with the stamps in it, and it made me angry because I thought it was wrong. It was laying a trip (in young people's parlance) on kids, placing a burden of obligation on them, as if not having your stamps made you a failure of some kind.

I suppose there was something of the personal in it, because when we came back from Minneapolis and I clocked into the DR Sunday School in Pinelands, I didn't have all the stamps I should have had. The DR Church is not all that big in Minneapolis and I'm not sure that any other kind of church stamp would have been good enough. In any case, there wasn't too much I could do about it, but I had a hard time because of the blanks in my book.

Looking back, I'm not certain how hard a time a 'hard time' really was. At the time, though, it was very real to me. Now I wonder if the 'trip' doesn't work two ways, and whether by taking it to heart I hadn't been the one who laid the trip on myself.

My husband Kobus was much smarter than I was. When he was a child, Kobus was ill. He had a condition called Purphy's disease. He was in Michaelis Orthopaedic Hospital for all of Grades 1 and 2 and couldn't attend church either, but it didn't faze him. His church had little stars or something like that, and what he did – instead of, like me, trying to explain himself when no one really wanted to listen – was to get out his own stars and forge a 'fully paid up' book so that he wouldn't need to explain.

At Sunday School we were all dressed up, which means you have to wear shoes and your socks scratch and you've got lots of buttons and there's a little bit of starch here and there and you have to carry a little handbag and stand still.

I couldn't wait for the minister to say the final blessings and get to the last amen. It's a terrible thing to say, but in that moment of release I actually thought, 'Thank heaven, now I know there probably is a God!' It was all so horribly boring that I couldn't wait to get out of there.

Then something happened to me that shouldn't happen to any self-respecting Calvinist girl. I discovered the *Roomse Gevaar*, which, loosely translated, means 'The Dangers of Catholicism'. Being worried about being overrun by the Catholics was a big thing in Afrikaner life and people were genuinely apprehensive. They worried about a lot of things, if you think about it now.

They wanted more white people to come to the country because the blacks were so many and the whites were so few on the ground, but they didn't want Catholics. Everyone knows that Catholics don't believe in birth control. First they breed like flies and then they run around converting people and before you've turned around you don't even have to worry about the blacks because you have a bigger problem on your hands. Catholics were definitely not good news and there were all kinds of rules and regulations to keep them in check, but my friend Dene Friedmann from Zeekoevlei was Catholic. She was my first Catholic friend and she was devout. I watched Dene, who is a friend of my heart to this day, and I wondered what it was she'd done to get things so organised.

When we were out of Cape Town skiing somewhere like the Clanwilliam dam, for example, Dene was meant on a Sunday to go to the nearest Catholic church. It was a question of kilometres and Dene worked it all out very carefully – where the church was, where the dam was and how many kilometres inbetween. If the church was a certain number of kilometres away you had to go, but if it was even half a kilometre further it was considered too far and you didn't have to go and you were forgiven. It seemed to me very sensible.

Sometimes I went with her to her church and I liked that too. Clothes weren't important. All we had to do was roll up our trousers and put a coat on and it didn't matter what it looked like.

Once you get there, it's hard not to like the Catholic Church. I suppose that's what all those old Afrikaner patriarchs were so worried about. I would have been a great problem to them. I liked it very much. I liked the 'smells and bells' and people moving around the church and jumping up to take Communion. Most of all, I liked how quick it was. One, two, three, it was over and you were free to go about your own business. It really impressed me.

At a later stage of my life I thought how wonderful it would be to be a nun, although I didn't go as far as asking for brochures about going into a nunnery. This had nothing to do with my having met the Pope, which I had.

When my father was meeting the rich and the famous I sometimes felt like chipping in and saying: 'Excuse me, but did you know that he isn't the first Barnard to have met the Pope?'

In fact, I did more than just meet Pope Paul. I actually stayed in his Summer Residence, the Castelgandolfo. It was the most fantastic place and I really did stay there, but I have to be absolutely honest and say I wasn't exactly the only guest. The house had been offered as accommodation for the competing teams in the European championships that year.

We did meet our host more formally on that visit and he blessed us, and all I can remember about the blessing is that I couldn't wait for it to be over because I had a tickle in my throat and couldn't stop coughing. So, it wasn't perhaps the profoundly life changing moment it might have been. It was certainly not that meeting that turned my thoughts towards how very nice it might be to be a nun.

The peace of it all was very attractive to me. I was no longer the girl-wonder waterskier. I was growing up and beginning to see that the adult world held problems more complex than being up to scratch for competitive skiing and having to find, somewhere inside yourself, that special edge that was supposed to make you a winner.

My parents were divorced and possibly as a result of that, but then again perhaps not, I could see nothing at all wrong with the single life. I liked the idea of the nunnery and the bells pealing away the segments of the day, leaving you free to go out from that community into the broader community and do that work you wanted to do. Of course, that didn't happen to me.

I have mentioned our special family friend, Father Tom Nicholson, more than once in these pages. He's been there for every crisis in the Barnard family.

He was there when my brother died. He comforted my father when he and Barbara divorced. Barbara was Catholic, and when she died he conducted the service for her, and her ashes are kept in his parish church in the Cape Town suburb of Plumstead. Father Tom officiated at my father's wedding to Karin. In short, he has been a friend to us all.

In terms of nationality, Father Tom is an Irishman. He comes from Galway in Eire. In terms of ordination, he is Roman Catholic. In terms of his vision, he is a man with a view as big as the whole wide world, with love and wisdom enough to encompass everyone.

Most of the time Father Tom comes to see us just as our friend. On more formal occasions he puts on what his friend Kate, who is one hundred years old, calls his Come to Jesus Collar and acts in his official capacity.

When we went to the airport on the day my father came home from Paphos and we were all at the airport waiting for him, Father Tom was there too, and he wore his Come to Jesus Collar and gave a blessing and it was a simple thing. It would have pleased my father.

18

What happened next

The same thing that always happens.
The past moved away from us and
we went on with our lives

What happened next after the death of my father is exactly what happens to most people, which is to say, life goes on. But something else too: the landscape of my life was changed; it was inescapably different. One day, while I wasn't looking, my children had grown up. My son, Tiaan, is at the University of Stellenbosch studying law and my daughter, Karen, is studying part-time while making shoes. She's a wonderfully free spirit. She likes to try new things.

Three people whose lives were a major part of the time I have written about are no longer with us. My father, my brother and beautiful Barbara are all gone, as if we dreamed them. As if they were here for a moment, lighting up the world and making it warmer and better, and then they were gone.

It's sad when someone young and beautiful like Barbara dies. When Christiaan officially opened his Design Centre in Newlands, Cape Town, I looked at him and his brother Frederick, the two sons Barbara had given my father, and wished she had been given more time with them. I know it's what she would have wished herself.

It occurred to me also that the boys were now really alone. They had lost both their parents; Ulli, their grandmother, whom my father held in great affection, was gone; and shortly after she died, Barbara's father, Fred Zoellner, died too. It was a very hard thing for them and for their little sister, Bianca.

I remembered the first time I'd seen Barbara and how exquisite I'd thought she was. I remember going out for dinner with her and my father, being introduced by them to grappa, which was the big thing in those days. She and my father had many happy years together. In their time together he was probably in the prime of his life: he was at the peak of his powers and the focus of a great deal of world attention, while the financial problems that had plagued him as they plague all up and coming young doctors had begun to melt away.

I suppose if you could single out any time in his life that was truly glorious, then this must have been that time, and Barbara, who was so greatly admired by everyone who met her, was the perfect person to share it with.

The age difference didn't seem to worry her at all. Sometimes when we visited at their home my father would make a joke. He'd say his foot had gone to sleep and he was going to join it and we'd all laugh and Barbara would go off and fetch another bottle of wine and suggest that we let him have his rest and stay a little longer and visit with her.

It wasn't something I would have said to Barbara but the reality was that my father was, it had to be faced, a little older. He needed his sleep.

When I married, the wedding reception was at my father's restaurant, La Vita. Kobus and I were living in Durban at the time and Barbara arranged everything. My father's friend Sid Cywes, who was an orchid grower, lent 30 pots of orchids to decorate the venue and it was really a very happy, informal affair. Just the kind of thing I like.

As a treat my father arranged a suite at the President Hotel on the seafront in Cape Town for us and a wonderful room at Matjiesfontein, the perfect little Victorian village in the Karoo. It was the old magician at work again!

My father said: 'It was a very splendid event and my daughter radiated happiness. I have to admit that I was so very happy for her that I got slightly drunk that evening.'

I think we all felt slightly delirious. The wedding was a great success. My mother was there and she looked wonderful in an out-fit by Elzbieta Rosenwerth. My wedding had brought our family together, which was not usual in those days. In my heart I suppose I knew it was an illusion, but it was wonderful while it lasted. Even today, with my father gone and Barbara too, when I think back to that day we are all still there in our places, with me in my wedding finery about to become Mrs Kobus Visser, and a feeling of gold still lingers around all of it.

Although they had both remarried, my father always retained his interest in and affection for Barbara. When she told him she'd been diagnosed with cancer he immediately set about finding out what could be done to help her. No one knew better than he did how quickly research moves. There are always advances being made in research, new drugs being developed all the time. He spent a great deal of time and immense amounts of energy, and I'm quite sure used his name for all it was worth, to try to find something that could help.

It was no good. Barbara was very ill and the illness was termi-nal. She died as she'd lived, quietly and in a dignified way. Towards the end she would see very few people other than the priest.

My father was devastated at Barbara's funeral. He wept inconsolably, like a child. His great friend Emiliano, of the La Vita restaurant days, the scene of so many good times and parties including my own wedding, put his arms around him to comfort him. I knew that because of all that had passed between Barbara and him, because of all the happy memories he must have had of her, in that moment of final parting my father was beyond comfort.

He said of Barbara afterwards that she had been 'one of the' loves of his life, but my father was always a gentleman. My own view is that in Barbara my father found a particular mixture of attributes that was exactly right for him.

As for me, I was still busy working with 'my' children and as usual, although quite by chance, my children led me into what was to be the next phase of my life as Mrs Kobus Visser.

When I was in my first official teaching post at Monterey, where Barbara's boys were at school, I took my class on a school outing to see the Simon's Town docks. (You see, there I was, quite grown up and still hanging around boats – although in this case, warships and not cruise liners.)

It was, I can see now, an overambitious thing to have done with a group of four- and five-year olds who are full of energy for just about anything but get tired quickly.

Simon's Town is home to the naval base on the Indian Ocean side of the Cape Peninsula. The train ride there is exciting in itself because the track runs along the sea for most of the way. The children were in high spirits and the day went well. There were fifteen of them, from which you may deduce that I was very young and very optimistic. By the time we were ready to leave for home they were flagging a bit, and it's quite a long walk from the dockyard to the station. The walk soon became a trudge and I was marching doggedly along, carrying one of the smaller ones piggyback.

A young naval rating came over to me and asked if I was

Deirdre Barnard. I said yes. He said he was Gerhard Visser and he'd known me from my university days and from the days when I was a waterskier.

'Come to lunch at our house on Sunday,' I said.

That's me, you see, and I didn't really think he'd come, but he did, and we all liked him and invited him to come any time he liked and he did that too. He was from Pretoria and doing his national service in the navy at Simon's Town. Everyone felt sorry for the national servicemen. They got conscripted and had to do training. Many of them were sent far from their homes. Any ideas of further education had to be put on hold while they offered up first a year and then two years to the pleasure of the state, who were training them 'to stave off the Communist onslaught'.

I don't know about Communist onslaught, but I do know about the navy. I had been to Simon's Town dockyard with my class and seen the extent of what it had to offer; and all I can say is that from what I'd heard, the Communist onslaught when it eventually arrived was going to be pretty big, and so were the Atlantic and Indian oceans. In the light of this, after what I saw of the navy, I didn't have very much hope for the game plan.

In any case, for the duration of his service Gerhard was a friend of our house, and it was our pleasure to have him there. Later, after he'd returned home, I took my grandmother up to Pretoria to visit my mother, who lived there in those days. It was one of 'those' visits. You will know what I mean. I was happy to be with my mother and grandmother but I was young, the days were long and I was spending them knitting and doing crochet, both worthy occupations for a third generation Calvinist girl, but to be honest it gets a bit much.

I thought I'd give Gerhard a ring and tell him I was in town and would like to see him. He said fine, he'd like that, and could he bring his little brother Kobus along?

I was 28 years old. As far as I know the option for entering the nunnery stays open until just about any age, but I now knew it was never going to be an option for me.

When I came back to my mother's flat that day and her neighbour asked who I'd gone out with, I said 'the man I'm going to marry', and so it turned out, and even geography played along. Kobus was a teacher in those days at Paul Roos Gymnasium, a school in Stellenbosch at a very convenient courting distance from where I lived.

Kobus is wonderful. We have similar roots, which counts for a lot. Kobus grew up in Usakos, which is also in Namibia, that same big, dry place (not exactly 'Waterworld') where my mother grew up. He has some very entertaining stories to tell. In their town the town hall served as the 'bioscope', the cinema. To book your seat for the once-a-week show you had to get there early in the day and put an item of clothing on the seat and everyone would know the seat was reserved.

We are not talking Pucci or Elzbieta or even Ninon boutique garments here! Usakos is a small place and poor, but even so, people like to show themselves off a bit and bioscope night is a good night to do it on, because everyone will be there and everyone will see.

We call Kobus's mother Ouma Annie, and on the Night of the New Twin-Set which Ouma Annie had knitted herself, she sent Kobus's brother Quinton to the bioscope on his bicycle to book their seats and make sure her seat was reserved with the new twin-set.

How it works is that once you've taken your seat and seen the first half of the show, at interval, before the main attraction, you stand up out of your seat and slip into the new clothing item so that everyone can get a good look. Unfortunately, on the Night of the New Twin-Set it was not destined to work out quite as planned.

Poor Quinton! He put the twin-set in the carrier bag of his bike and somewhere between home and the bioscope a piece of wool from the sleeve got caught in the spoke of his bicycle. By the time he realised something was wrong, the entire sleeve had unravelled. Honesty, we all know, is the best policy, but Quinton had to think on his feet and he thought about Ouma Annie and what would be coming his way if he owned up. So he thought about it and decided that honesty being the best policy was all well and good as a general rule, but maybe not in this particular case.

They all went to the show. Ouma Annie picked up her new twin-set off the seat and at interval, when the big moment came, she put on the cardigan minus a sleeve.

It's a family legend, a fireside tale of small towns and small town people who are kind and courteous, who cherish their stories, are generous with their time and such gifts as they have, and find their pleasures in very small things.

That suits me. It's the way my own heart lies, and so you could say that in this way, as well as in so many others, Kobus was actually perfect for me.

Kobus is genuinely interested in everyone he meets and can talk to anyone at all. Also, he started out as a teacher, which echoes my own great passion for working with children.

I know it wasn't easy for him, marrying a Barnard. We have what you might call a rather complicated family dynamic. He knew that, but I don't think he could have realised the full enormity of it until he actually lived through all he has lived through with me.

What would I ever have done without him? I really don't know. He's been everything one could wish for in a husband and father and a great deal more than that. Tolerant, long-suffering and kind are just three words that come to mind. There are plenty of others.

My father called me 'restless'. He talked about my 'wandering around the world skiing' and not settling down. I think one of the reasons he got 'slightly drunk' at my wedding was out of relief. He liked Kobus very much. He considered him a solid, down-to-earth Afrikaner. Personally, I think Kobus is rather more than that, but to give him a few more adjectives to make my father happy is all right with me. I suppose both he and my mother must have had a few bad moments wondering about exactly the kind of man I might present them with one day. Given my habit for accumulating people, some of whom my parents were a bit dubious about, Kobus must have come as a pleasant surprise.

As I've already said, marrying a Barnard is not for the fainthearted. You need hair on your teeth and all these many years and two wonderful children later, I really can't imagine a life spent with anyone else.

I've been told that I have two sides. On the one hand I am strong and capable. On the other I am an absolute child. That's official, and it's me in a few words. I don't disagree. I'm just not quite sure what one does about it. An analyst will tell you that what you need to do is take a good look at these separate components of yourself and integrate them.

I know it doesn't always make things easy for the people closest to me and all I can say – which is nothing new, it's something they hear all the time – is that I'm working on it.

My openness can infringe on other people's privacy. I realise that. Kobus and my children have borne the brunt of this. Tiaan's irritation with 'hullo, hullo' is probably just a nice way of pointing out that I'm a good talker, that what I need to learn is to keep quiet and listen.

I really do need to stop sometimes, to put the brakes on and fully recognise that it's all right to pull up the drawbridge and just be a family together. Sometimes you just need to be a married couple together and sometimes you need to be able to be by yourself.

I think about my mother. I have always been protective of my father. I never felt that way about my mother. It never occurred to me that there was anything that could happen in life that my mother couldn't cope with. When my mother went through the divorce and that bad time in my life there was nothing inside me that said I ought to be carrying pain for her. I suppose that is strange. I know it's unfair, but it's how I felt. 'But mothers don't conk in', was about as far as I got. My poor mother. I should really have been able to do better than that.

What I can say about my mother is that such strengths and ability for fortitude I may have I got from her. I think that in the Afrikaner tradition women are meant to be the strong ones. It's accepted they should be and no one gives them any credit when they are. I think that sometimes even my mother, who's no slouch when it comes to telling people they've gone far enough, does things to please me. I'm perfectly sure there are times when I push the limits and am not sensitive enough to her boundaries.

I'm sure the same was true of my father too. There must have been times when I was invasive and difficult and extremely trying. I kept thinking I could help him in some way when really, I couldn't. I even thought that perhaps a little analysis might have been a good thing for him. That was the reason I kept trying to slip him the self-help books. I thought it might be a first step towards getting him to find someone professional to whom he could unburden himself, but my father didn't want to 'unravel'. No amount of persuasion, overt or covert, was going to persuade him to do so, and that was his right. I had no business trying to decide what might or might not be good for him.

I have a feeling inside me that I can't find a proper English word for. In Afrikaans we call it *onvergenoed*, which means 'being unable to be fulfilled, unable to be satisfied'. I think it was the same for my father.

When one has had the young life I had, when one has been the total focus of one parent and all the rules have been bent to make one happy, what comes after is very difficult to come to terms with.

In that first part of my life the constraints that applied to my peer group didn't apply to me. I was allowed to be out of school for three or four months at a time. I was allowed to spend most of my time doing the thing I was best at. When I wasn't training – and the training really was extremely demanding and took lots of time – my world was bursting with adventure.

I travelled and met new people. In these circumstances you feel as if the world really is your oyster, that everything it yields up is good, that somehow you deserve it – and of course, because you're young, you think it will go on forever.

When it ends, as it must, what comes in its place is the most terrible kind of emptiness. Once you've got out from under the duvet and realised that you've still got a life to live, your knee-jerk reaction is to become incredibly demanding of the people around you. You do it because you have a huge gap to fill and you don't know how else to fill it.

Of course, it isn't fair. All you're doing is 'laying your trip on them'. You don't have the right to do that and the road back to finding yourself again is long and it's hard but it's the only way there is. There's no one and nothing that can fill that gap except you.

I think we should all step aside from our lives for a while and consider how many gifts we have that can help to fulfil us. There's so much love all around us, love that we overlook if we search after it too frantically when all we need do is be still and receive it by osmosis, along with all those other good things in the world.

All I can say is that I am trying to be better. I am trying to develop more of an interior life. The more I can live inside myself, the less I will stop invading other people's space. It doesn't matter if you do it for attention, for comfort or because you sincerely want to help. It's an invasion just the same and I'm working on it.

It's hard as far as my children are concerned. I know you have to let them go so that they can 'go through the process' for themselves. It's easy to write down. It's easy when you see it sitting on paper like that. In real life it's a very hard thing for a parent to do.

I have tried to make a safe haven for them as my mother did for me. My mother was protective. We were cared for, wrapped in cottonwool, you might say, because that was her way. I'm not quite sure though how well this prepares children for the wild world 'outside'.

Kobus and I have always kept 'open house' for our children and their friends. They know my feelings very well. Their father and I are in their lives 24 hours a day, every day of the year, whether we are actually physically there or not.

They are free to come to us and be with us just whenever they feel a need to. If they're ever in a jam we are only a telephone call away and we will come to them and fetch them wherever they are; and whatever kind of a jam they're in we will never be judgemental but will do all we can to help sort things out.

I do count my many blessings just as the old hymn instructs, but I see my fault lines as well. I keep thinking I can barge into other people's lives, take on their problems and somehow make things better for them, and of course, I can't.

That's a hard admission to make. I have, at times in my life, wanted to stand between my father and the world when I have felt the world has not been kind to him. There have been moments when I have felt such a feeling of tenderness and sadness toward my late brother that I really have found the pain of it too much to bear. He had so much love in his life, yet it seemed that something in him just made him unable to accept it. It was my old feeling again. That he was drifting away on an ice floe, unable to reach out and take all the care and nurturing that were his without him even having to ask.

I have learnt something in my life and that is that you can

absorb someone's pain all you like, but there's nothing you can do to take it away from them. All that will happen is that you burden yourself with it and that your burden affects those around you. At some point you simply have to let go.

The last time I saw my father was when I took him to the airport. He was going on a visit to Israel and then on the holiday trip to Paphos.

I had a sense of something out of place. I'd done the airport drop-off so many times in these last months of his life. My friends used to joke with me about it and ask why he couldn't take the shuttle like everyone else did. It would have been much easier. Certainly when it's a crack of dawn flight, as his last flight out of South Africa was, it would have made far more sense.

The truth is that I liked taking him to the airport. I liked the drive out and the two of us alone in the car. I'm tempted to say it was like old times, and it was in a way, and then again it wasn't.

We had our way of doing things. I'd draw up in the five-minute drop zone, he'd get a trolley and then we'd say our goodbyes and I'd go back to town.

I couldn't do it. It's quite still at the airport so early in the morning when it isn't really light yet. Even so, even though I'd pulled out from the kerb and out into the road on the homeward journey, something very strong inside me seemed to be telling me I had to go back. I wanted to say 'goodbye' to my father just one more time. I just had to do it.

I couldn't reverse into the oncoming traffic and it's not a good idea just to abandon a car. All my father needed was to hear on his first phone call back home that his car, a brand new acquisition of which he was exceedingly proud, had been towed away because some fanciful notion had got me in its grip. All the same, I had to go back.

It was so stupid. For all I knew my father might have got lucky and already checked in and gone into the departure hall. He'd think either I was nuts or he'd forgotten something vital in the car. I didn't care.

I got out of the car and left it just where it stood and went back, dashed back if you must know, looking for my father. I just had to see him. It was as simple as that.

In a way airports are not unlike hospitals. There's an antiseptic, impersonal feeling about them and the lights are too bright. There are cleaners about and they always seem to move very slowly at that time of the day and there's not too much of a buzz among passengers either. At that hour of the morning they're still half-asleep and even though there were not all that many of them, there were too many for me, so I couldn't see him immediately. I still had the terrible feeling he might have left without my seeing him; and then I did see him.

He was walking slowly, pushing his trolley as if it held all the burdens of the world in it, and he didn't see me and I stopped right where I was and just looked at him. An old man hunched over his trolley walking very slowly as if every step hurt.

I just couldn't bear it.

I knew how much his arthritis hurt. When he was on 'public display' he made every effort to hide the pain, but the truth is that he was in pain almost all the time and on that morning there was no attempt to hide it at all. I felt so sorry for him. I felt my heart shrink and slide up into my throat. I felt the way you feel when something terribly sad happens.

People moved between us and he still didn't see me.

I watched him move painfully into his place in the queue and then I forced myself to be myself and just rush up to him.

It wasn't the way we usually were, but if he thought it was odd, he didn't comment on it.

'It's nothing,' I said. 'I've just come to say goodbye to you. That's all.'

It was silly, of course. I'd already said goodbye to him in the drop-off zone. If he thought that was funny he never said that either.

What he did was something he rarely did. He turned to me and put his arms around me and they were the strong, safe arms of my childhood. I could see his hands, his famous hands gnarled now by arthritis. I could smell him and feel the rough texture of his jacket under my cheek and I could close my eyes for just a moment and feel complete.

'*Dankie, Didi,*' he said. '*Dankie vir alles. Ek is lief vir jou.*'
'Thank you, Didi. Thank you for everything. I love you.'

It was the last thing he said to me. I never saw my father again.

After my father died there was an avalanche of condolence letters. They came from all over the world, some of them from very famous people, some from people who hadn't known him personally at all. Some came from heads of state, from ambassadors, from people – some of them former patients of his – whose life he'd touched in some way.

I suppose, like the rest of my family, I was looking for some kind of comfort. People were very kind in what they said. A friend of his with whom he'd had an informal supper a few weeks before he died wrote:

> I had the opportunity to spend a quiet evening with him just a few weeks ago. He showed fatigue and was frail and it was as though he knew what was coming. Little did we know that this would be the last time we would see him.
>
> We spoke about so many things and he shared with us all his regrets, errors and aspirations. Of all your father's entire achievements the one characteristic we would like to remember him by is his honesty. A man that can stand up in public and private and admit to his shortcomings is brave

and courageous and for this we salute him. He often spoke about you and how he had neglected to give you the time and attention you deserved. He was so appreciative of all your love and devotion and he told us that the one person that came to his aid, unconditionally, was you. You were there for him when he needed love most.

I am not an only child. I was not the only child who suffered loss or who grieved for my father. I know that, but this letter came to me at a time when I really needed to read it. I could stand up right here and tell you all about my own shortcomings, but it was the word 'unconditionally' that touched me. I did love my father with all my heart, and sometimes after doing a lot of soul searching, sometimes after a great many tears, I always come back to that point at which I started. I loved my father in a very simple, straightforward way without any conditions at all. I would like to believe he knew that. I would like even more to believe that at the end of it all, he acknowledged to someone that he knew it and that he understood. As I told you, our family is a great many things but we are definitely not the best communicators on the planet. At least when it comes to communicating with each other.

I wouldn't be so arrogant as to say my life has been extraordinary. What I can say is that it isn't at all what I'd bargained on when I was the doctor's daughter growing up in Zeekoevlei.

That's on the one hand. On the other hand I have to think that and say 'so what?' Show me the person whose life actually turned out the way they expected? At least I can say of my own life that it's been lots of things but at least it's never been dull.

Once a year we have Barnard Day. Goodness knows we have more than enough public holidays in South Africa and this one isn't officially on the calendar and never will be, although it is on our family calendar.

It was Frederick's idea and we made a little oath in which we all promise to do our best to keep it up. Once a year on The Day of Reconciliation, as we call it, we all get together at Maureen Brink's house in Blouberg just outside Cape Town. So far it's worked very well.

Over the year's 'Auntie' Maureen lost the 'Aunt' part. That too came with the territory. As my father's wives became younger and more modern the respectful form of address, 'aunt' and 'uncle', which Afrikaans children use when they address their parents' friends, fell away. It seemed strange then for me to keep using it and so I let it drift quietly away too so that these 'older people', family friends of my childhood, suddenly became Joan and Maureen and Eileen to me.

I had to be careful around my father, too. As the wives became younger and I got older I began having a problem with 'Pappa' as well. It didn't seem to fit somehow, especially when I was with Karin and calling her husband Pappa.

I wasn't sure what to do about it. I couldn't very well call him Chris, so when there were people around and I had to call him something I just called him 'Mmm'.

My mother doesn't come to these gatherings and we respect her right to her own space. Her family, the Louws, are wonderful at keeping together. There are eighteen cousins in that family and they get together every three years at the original family farm, Keerweder, in Paarl, in the Cape winelands. The main force behind this is my mother's sister Aunt Nellie, a remarkable woman who is also my godmother (although that isn't what she's remarkable for!).

Before my father died we were planning a last holiday in Buffels Bay. Kobus and I go to Buffels Bay every summer. We rent a house there and this year we wanted my father to come and join us with Armin and Lara, and my mother would have been with us then.

After his separation from Karin my father had given the two smallest children a skiing holiday. Off they'd gone, along with an au pair to take care of them, but it hadn't been a success. My father was really getting too old for that kind of thing, which is why I suggested Buffels Bay to him. That way, I would be there to keep an eye on the children and there would be other children there for them to play with.

He agreed and we rented a house for him. We had all kinds of complicated arrangements in place to see everyone was comfortable. My mother was concerned that the house we'd chosen for my father and the children had too many steps for my father to negotiate safely. There was some talk about us swapping houses, but all of it came to nothing.

What I wanted was for Armin and Lara to have a sample of some of the joys my brother and I'd had as children on our wonderful holidays to that same place. I think they would have been happy there. I think my father would have enjoyed it, but unfortunately it was not to be because in September he died.

───

Our plan for Barnard Day is to include as many members of our creeping vine family as we can. Last year, Barbara's husband Joe Silva came too.

Karin remarried two years ago and has another child now but we hope in time she too may feel that she wants to come along and take up her place in our family, and I have a hope of my own. I hope that one day my mother might take up that place that is always there for her and will always be rightfully hers.

It is quite strange, in a way, sitting at that table looking around. Frederick, in particular, looks very much like our father but there are pieces of him in all the children and in the grandchildren too and we all have our place in the grand scheme of his life, and we all have our memories, but we all go our separate paths.

After everyone has gone home and I am alone with myself I see all the pieces of my life in front of me as if they were a jigsaw puzzle, each exactly the shape it should be, destined to slot neatly into each other piece until everything is complete.

I'm glad that life changes. I have enjoyed my highs to the full and disliked the painful parts just the same as anyone else would, but so far, it has been what one could call 'a life', and I wouldn't have changed any of it.

It's a strange feeling you have about those who are gone. It's like snipping a thread and seeing them drift off away from you, getting smaller and smaller, always looking the way you remember them most fondly.

My brother; beautiful Barbara with her slightly aloof manner and her lovely smile that lit up her face; and as for my father, what can I say about him that hasn't already been said? Except that, in my opinion, it isn't the beginning or end of his life that's important. What's impressive is its scope. He had a huge life and it went far beyond superficial glamour.

He's gone now, but while he was here he made magic. Even looking back I can see him. It was as I remembered it. There was something really special about him. At least there was for me. While he was here he shone. As I said earlier, he shone with a light so radiant it could make you feel sad.

Afterword

People who write books often have a dedication in them or an epi-gram that sums up what's coming in just a few well-chosen lines. I think that works for people who know in advance what they're going to say. I am not one of them. I am the same as I always am. It wasn't until I'd finished that I knew what I was going to say and now that it's done, something occurs to me.

What's important is not the loss of those that we love or our inability to keep them with us for even a while longer, no matter how much we might wish that we could. What's important is what they leave behind with us.

My father was an Afrikaner. Afrikaans was his mother tongue. He loved poetry and he liked to quote it. Everyone who knew him knew this. I would like then, before I too move on with my life to end in that place where other people begin.

I know that even though I am the Barnard Broadcasting Corporation I can't speak for us all, but as usual I have something to say – the last word, if you like, and I would like to say it in my father's language, in the voice of his people which always spoke directly to his heart.

This, then, is for my father, for my brother, Andre, and for Barbara.

Mits dese wil ons vir jou sê
hoe diep ons liefde vir jou lê.
(Boerneef)

With this we want to tell you
how deeply we love you.
(Boerneef)

Publications referred to

Barnard, Christiaan (1993). *Fifty Ways to a Healthy Heart.* Vlaeberg, Cape Town.

Barnard, Christiaan, and Pepper, Curtis Bill (1969). *One Life.* Tafelberg, Cape Town.

Barnard, Christiaan, ed. (2001 edn). *The Body Machine: Your Health in Perpective.* Thorsons, London.

Barnard, Louwtjie (1971). *Heartbreak.* Howard Timmins, Cape Town.

Cooper, David, ed. (1992). *Chris Barnard By Those Who Know Him.* Vlaeberg, Cape Town.